PETER F. NEUMEYER, editor of this volume in the *Twentieth Century Interpretations* series, is Assistant Professor of Education, Harvard Graduate School of Education. A distinguished critic on Kafka, Neumeyer has written for such literary journals as *The University Review, The Dalhousie Review, The German Quarterly,* and *Wisconsin Studies in Contemporary Literature.*

TWENTIETH CENTURY INTERPRETATIONS OF

THE CASTLE

A Collection of Critical Essays

Edited by

PETER F. NEUMEYER

Prentice-Hall, Inc.  *Englewood Cliffs, N. J.*

 Library of Congress Catalog Card Number 69-11356. Printed in the United States of America.

Current printing (last number):
10 9 8 7 6 5 4 3 2 1

Prentice-Hall International, Inc. (*London*)

Contents

Introduction

by Peter F. Neumeyer

I

Franz Kafka (1883–1924) was younger than either Thomas Mann (1875–1955) or William Somerset Maugham (1874–1965). Had he not succumbed to tuberculosis, and had he avoided the fate his three sisters met at the hands of the Nazis in a concentration camp, he might be alive today. We will attempt to review some of the more significant events of his brief and outwardly uneventful life, with the reservation that in Kafka's life, perhaps more than in most, much is not what it seems.

Kafka was born on July 3, 1883, in the city of Prague, then part of the Austro-Hungarian Empire. He was the son of a strong, vigorous, dominating father, who was a self-made businessman, and of a rather mellow and contemplative mother. To be a German-Jew in Prague at the time meant that one was part of a national and cultural minority, though certainly it did not necessarily mean that one was poor. "The German Jew in Prague was an industrialist, a prosperous businessman, a leading bank official. . . . Almost all wholesale merchandising and almost all import and export trade was carried on by Jews." [1] But prosperity notwithstanding, the Jews (and in fact all Germans) were isolated in a sort of spiritual ghetto. Kafka too was of the cultural minority: he attended German elementary schools, and then the German university in Prague; he heard his lectures in German, and usually spoke German, though his acquaintance, Gustav Janouch, reports that he spoke it with something like a Czech accent.[2]

[1] Pavel Eisner, *Franz Kafka and Prague* (New York: Golden Griffin Books, Arts Inc., 1950), p. 22.

[2] Gustav Janouch, *Gespräche mit Kafka* (Frankfurt am Main: S. Fischer Verlag, 1951), p. 21. For further information about Kafka's national origins, about Prague, and about the status of German Jews in that city, see Meno Spann, "The Minor Kafka Problem," *The Germanic Review,* XXXII (October, 1957), 163–77. Heinz Politzer, "Prague and the Origins of R. M. Rilke, F. Kafka, and F. Werfel," *Modern Language Quarterly,* XVI (March, 1955), 49–62.

At Prague's German university, Kafka first studied chemistry for a very short time, then became interested in *Germanistik* (German Literature and Philology), but soon turned to Law as being the least constricting. It was in Law that he obtained the degree of *Doktor Juris* in 1906.[3]

At the university, in 1902–3, Kafka met his lifelong friend, Max Brod, who was to be his literary executor and principal biographer. Brod reports that already in those university years Kafka was writing, but did not think highly of his own work, and that he had wanted to destroy the still extant "Description of a Struggle," which he read aloud to Brod in 1910.[4] Even so early we may note traces in that sketch of what were to become the characteristics of his mature work: the heightening of the mundane, the sharp focus on seemingly trivial everyday incidents, and the precise detail which, by the very clarity with which it is perceived, acquires uniqueness and import.[5]

In 1907, having served a brief apprenticeship in the criminal courts of Prague, and always looking for a job that would leave as many hours as possible free for his writing, Kafka went to work for a time in the private business offices of the Assicurazioni Generali. In 1908 he took up what was to be his lifetime employment in the quasi-governmental offices of the Workers' Accident Insurance Institute of the Kingdom of Bohemia. There his task consisted largely of evaluating the claims of groups of workers who were petitioning for reclassification in a higher insurance-risk category. There still survive several papers meticulously and conscientiously prepared by Kafka, in which he analyzed closely and described with sympathy the dangerous manual operations in which his worker-clients were engaged. Though it would be stretching a point to say that we clearly see the hand of the novelist in these technical papers, we may argue with some plausibility that we do find traces of Kafka's concern with accident-prevention engineering in the description of the diabolical machine of his story, *In the Penal Colony* (1919).

[3] The degree *Doktor Juris* was the most common university degree in Central Europe at the time, says John Urzidil. *Menorah Journal,* XXXI (October–December, 1943), 276.

[4] Many Kafka manuscripts, perhaps some early ones, were lost when the Gestapo raided the Berlin home of Kafka's friend, Dora Dymant.

[5] These are characteristics which Kafka had found admirable in Hofmannsthal's "Chandos letter," and his recently published "Conversation Regarding Poetry," from which he singled out the vivid image, "the smell of damp stones in a hallway," calling it to the special attention of Max Brod. Klaus Wagenbach, *Kafka* (Hamburg: Rowohlt Taschenbuch Verlag, 1964), p. 42.

In all the years of employment with the Insurance Institute, it seems to have been a constant battle for Kafka to squeeze, push, and juggle the hours of employment in such a way as to obtain time for writing. Moreover, as he worked on his diaries and his numerous stories and sketches all the while, we have the testimony of his acquaintances that he was modestly gregarious, and a good, loyal, friend, and that he found time to listen, and to assist those who came to him for encouragement. Gustav Janouch's reconstruction, *Conversations with Kafka,* reveals the wise and gentle manner in which Kafka received the engaging, but highly emotional youngster, despite his own intense absorption during these years in writing *The Castle.*[6]

In addition to these occupations and preoccupations, there was the increasing distraction throughout his life from insomnia and from frightful headaches which he once described as being the sort of feeling a pane of glass must have in the spot where it cracks.[7] Add, too, the miseries attendant on his tuberculosis, diagnosed in 1917, and then also the deep inner turmoil occasioned by three engagements (two to the same young lady)—and it seems remarkable how much writing he did, in fact, produce. Some measure of the spiritual disruption his private affairs caused him is shown in his now published letters to Milena Jesenská, dating from 1920, the year in which he had broken an engagement with Julie Wohryzek. Milena Jesenská was a strong, courageous, Christian young woman who was already married to a learned, but callously egotistical husband. The voluminous correspondence Kafka carried on with her is of particular interest because it dates from those years in which Kafka was writing *The Castle.*

The year 1922 was significant for Kafka. His tuberculosis took a decided turn for the worse. In March, he read to Max Brod for the first time from the beginnings of *The Castle.* He finally broke off his agonized relationship with Milena, and soon thereafter, while undergoing a health cure at a Baltic resort, met the charming and loyal Dora Dymant. She remained with him for the next two years, faithfully looked after him, and accompanied him to the sanatorium at Kierling, near Vienna, where on June 3, 1924 he died at the age of forty-one.

[6] Gustav Janouch, *Conversations with Kafka,* trans. Goronwy Rees (New York: Frederick A. Praeger, Inc., 1953).

[7] Max Brod, *Franz Kafka: A Biography,* second edition, trans. G. Humphreys Roberts and Richard Winston (New York: Schocken Books, 1963), p. 74.

Many of Kafka's short sketches and novellas had been published before his death, so that he was not without honor in his own short lifetime. As early as 1912 Brod had brought Kafka together with Ernst Rowohlt and Kurt Wolff, the sensitive and enlightened publishers who were instrumental in the publication of many of the more experimental authors, and who showed an interest in Kafka's work as well. Over Kafka's protests the short volume, *Betrachtung* (*Contemplation*), was published in a limited edition in December of that year. Other occasional publications followed, and a few public readings. The high esteem of his publishers is made clear in a letter dated November 3, 1921, in which Kurt Wolff urges him to send more of his writing, saying in part:

> None of the authors with whom we are connected comes to us with wishes or questions so seldom as you do, and with none of them do we feel that the outward fate of their published books is a matter of such indifference as with you. . . . From the bottom of my heart may I assure you that I personally have such a feeling for you and your work as I have only in the case of perhaps two or at most three of the writers whom we . . . are permitted to bring before the public.[8]

Wolff did, in fact, continue as Kafka's publisher, bringing out the three unfinished novels, *The Trial, The Castle,* and *America,* in 1925, 1926, and 1927 respectively, all against the author's expressed wishes. Max Brod, who took the initiative in this posthumous publication explains in his biography of Kafka that in those last years, especially at the end, when he had the friendship of Dora Dymant, and was reading Hebrew, the novelist was so happy and took such a renewed interest in life that "I . . . gathered the courage to regard as no longer valid his written instructions to me—written long before this period—which forbade the publication of any of his posthumous papers." [9]

Brod's decision has generally been thought wise. Kafka, for all his diffidence, was indeed held in high esteem at the time of his death, and Brod says correctly that "the voices of Hugh Walpole, Huxley, Bennett, André Gide, Herman Hesse, Buber, Thomas Mann, Heinrich Mann, Werfel, and many others writing in German, French, Dutch, Czech, Polish, Italian, and Hebrew, in England and America, united

[8] Brod, *Biography,* p. 136.
[9] Brod, *Biography,* p. 198.

in explaining Kafka's importance. . . . His works have appeared in all these languages, and awakened admiration." [10]

Professor Meno Spann reports that already in 1926 (the year *The Castle* was published) Kafka was included for study in Professor Hermann Pongs' seminar on German *novelle* at the University of Marburg, and that in the next year he was discussed in several German literary histories.[11] Henry Hatfield writes that "no one who has written in German in the twentieth century has had a greater impact on European literature than . . . Franz Kafka." [12] In our own time, "Kafkaesque" has become a cliché of criticism, applied often to writers like Beckett or Albee; and "theater of the absurd" and "black comedy" are terms popularly thought to have their spiritual antecedents in his works.[13] Perhaps the only censure of Kafka—historically interesting—was written during the Nazi interregnum, in such oddities as Hans Galinsky's *Deutsches Schrifttum der Gegenwart in der Englischen Nachkriegzeit* (1938) [*Contemporary German Writing in Postwar England*], which speaks of "Jewish work in the German langauge," "the Jewish stylist, Kafka," and "literary Judaism domiciled in Germany." [14]

II

The Castle is Kafka's last major book. For all its labyrinthian and prolix involutions, the plot of this not-quite-completed story (which Brod calls "that prodigious ballad of the homeless stranger who vainly strives to establish roots in the home of his choice") [15] is not difficult. One wintry night the protagonist, simply called K. (though the book had originally been begun in the first person), arrives in a snowy village dominated by the castle of Count Westwest. To the villagers at the local inn, K. declares himself to be the surveyor sent

[10] Brod, *Biography*, p. 213.

[11] *The Germanic Review*, XXXII (October, 1957), 164.

[12] Henry Hatfield, *Modern German Literature: The Major Figures in Context* (London: Edward Arnold [Publishers] Ltd., 1966), p. 84.

[13] For further consideration of Kafka's influence, especially in England, see Peter Demetz, "Kafka in England," *German Life and Letters*, IV (October, 1950), 12–30; also P. Neumeyer, "Kafka and England," *The German Quarterly*, XL (November, 1967), 630–42.

[14] (München), pp. 467, 468, 450.

[15] Brod, *Biography*, p. 219.

for by the Castle, and the remaining four hundred and fifty pages are devoted to his repeated attempts to be admitted to it. He takes into his service two men sent by the Castle, men who claim to be his old assistants, although both K. and the ostensible assistants, Arthur and Jeremiah, seem to know that they are not. Not long thereafter K. receives a message from Klamm, an official at the Castle, which is brought to him by Barnabas, a strange creature with whose sisters, Olga and Amalia, K.'s destiny becomes deeply involved. K. now takes up residence at the village school with Frieda, former mistress of Klamm. We learn, in a long subplot, of the case of Olga's sister Amalia, who, in refusing to respond to the improper solicitations by a representative of the Castle, had subjected her family to public scorn. Brod has compared the immoral demand by the Castle authority to God's humanly incomprehensible order that Abraham sacrifice his son, Isaac—a tale exemplifying the paradoxical incompatibility of the categories of morality and those of religion. And indeed, Kafka had, at the time, been reading that Biblical story as it is told and retold in Kierkegaard's *Fear and Trembling*.[16] As the novel draws to a close, K. is still engaged in repeated, nightmare-like attempts to reach the Castle. We know that these efforts will never succeed, but that eventually, worn down by the attempt, K. is to lie on his deathbed and—so Kafka told it to his friends—there finally receive word that he is not to be given access to the Castle itself, but will be permitted to live at peace in the village.

Such a summary does not do justice to the book, for what Kafka was saying in this story, however debatable its ultimate meaning may be, is evinced as much by the manner of the telling as by the plot. Moreover, anyone attempting to reproduce the plot makes implicit judgments on the meaning simply by what he chooses to recall or to emphasize. The enormous diversity of interpretations to which Kafka's simple narrative has given rise is suggested by the spectrum of opinions represented in the following essays.

III

Like any novel, *The Castle* derives both from its author's personal and psychological experience and from the temper of the time in which it came to be written. Beginning with Kafka's own experiences,

[16] Professor Heller notes the basic antitheses between the two stories (see pp. 77–78 below). Compare the essay by Professor Politzer (pp. 51–52).

we must note first that it was customary in German secondary schools such as the one Kafka attended to read a work titled *The Grandmother,* by the Czech writer, Bozena Nemcova. Max Brod has called our attention to Kafka's acknowledged debt to this mid-nineteenth-century idyllic pastoral novel, as well as to Kafka's related diary entry for June 11, 1914, a twelve-page sketch titled "Temptation in the Village," which "describes the tragedy of a man who wishes to live in a village with other people but is unable to become rooted in the strange place and to find his way to the Castle which looms forebodingly over the village." [17]

Three years later, in 1917, closer to the date of the actual composition of *The Castle,* misfortune struck. Kafka's lungs—as he perceptively put it—"conspired with my brain behind my back." [18] He suffered his first serious tubercular attacks, and, in an attempt to regain his strength by a therapeutic health regimen, he withdrew to a small estate in the mountains at Zürau. There he stayed until the summer of 1918, making brief, occasional, and unsuccessful attempts to return to work. He read Kierkegaard (which as stated above, may have left its traces in the Amalia sections of *The Castle*); he studied Hebrew; he spent time gardening; and he became acquainted for the first time with what might be called "country life"—a life evoked in some of the more rural settings of *The Castle.* (We must recall, though, that the first actual reference to the book is Max Brod's recollection of Kafka's reading from it on March 15, 1922.) [19]

Further and quite remarkable evidence of the state of Kafka's spirits during the years he spent writing *The Castle* can be found. After much misadventure and ill fortune, Gustav Janouch in 1947 made public his recollections of the conversations he had with Kafka between 1920 and 1922.[20] Shortly after the appearance of the Janouch

[17] "*The Castle*: Its Genesis," trans. Gerhard H. Weiss, in *Franz Kafka Today,* ed. Angel Flores and Homer Swander (Madison: University of Wisconsin Press, 1962), p. 161.

[18] Wagenbach, *Kafka,* p. 108.

[19] Brod, *Biography,* pp. 185–86. Two more immediate inspirations which Heinz Politzer suggests for Kafka's castle and the tortuous path leading to it are the actual castle of Rudolf II on the Hradžany Hill, near which Kafka lived one winter, and the seventeenth-century treatise, *The Labyrinth of the World and the Paradise of the Heart,* by the Czech philosopher, Jan Amos Komensky (Comenius). *Franz Kafka: Parable and Paradox,* revised, expanded edition (Ithaca: Cornell University Press, 1966), pp. 232–33.

[20] Janouch, *Conversations.* The "conversations," written down shortly after they allegedly took place, were considered plausible by Dora Dymant and by Max Brod. There exists a second, as yet unpublished manuscript by Gustav Janouch, which Janouch claims to be the second half of the first "conversations."

volume, Willi Haas published the moving collection of letters written by Kafka, also during the years of composition of *The Castle,* to Milena Jesenská.[21]

Reading these conversations and letters, one is inclined to believe Brod when he says that Kafka had incorporated into the novel many of the dilemmas which plagued him while writing it. Brod maintains that we are to see Milena herself clearly caricatured in the person of Frieda, and that in the cruel and arbitrary Klamm we have "an exaggerated and demonized image of Milena's legal husband, from whom she could not completely break away emotionally."[22] It is certainly true, at the very least, that Kafka's experience was of a piece with what he wrote. Thus, in *The Castle,* the protagonist strives vainly, incessantly, obsessively, and compulsively; any enterprise he assays is undertaken first from one point of attack, then from another; and the outcome seems, by the nature of the task, of the striving, perhaps even of the cosmos, to be foredoomed to failure. This situation and theme may be traced throughout the work of Kafka—for example (in slightly different form), in *The Trial,* and in the short story of the man pleading vainly at the Gate of the Law in *The Country Doctor* (1919). And they recur too in his life. Thus he writes, broodingly, to Milena in one letter:

> Here I sit in front of the Director's door, the Director is away, but I wouldn't be surprised if he were to come out and say: "I don't like you, either, that's why I'm giving you notice." "Thank you," I'd say, "I need this urgently for a trip to Vienna." "So?" he'd say, "now I like you again and I withdraw the notice." "Oh," I'd say, "now I can't take the trip." "Oh yes," he'd say, "for now again I don't like you, so I give you notice." And so it would be an endless story.[23]

And Milena, in turn, writes, describing Kafka to Max Brod:

> Have you ever gone to a post office with him? After he has filed away a telegram and then, shaking his head, picked out the window he likes best, and after he has tramped from one window to the next, without in the least understanding why and wherefore until he finally stumbles on the right one, and after he has paid and received his change—he counts up what he has received, finds that he has been given a crown too much, and returns the crown to the girl at the window. Then he walks slowly

[21] Franz Kafka, *Briefe an Milena* (Frankfurt am Main: S. Fischer Verlag, 1952); *Letters to Milena,* ed. Willi Haas, trans. Tania and James Stern (New York: Schocken Books, 1953).

[22] Brod, *Biography,* p. 220.

[23] *Letters to Milena,* p. 129.

away, counts his change again, and on the last step down to the street he sees that the returned crown did belong to him after all. Now you stand helplessly beside him—he shifts his weight from one foot to the other and ponders what he ought to do. To go back is hard; there is a crowd at the windows upstairs, "Then let it be," I say. He looks at me in utter horror. How can you let it be? Not that he cares about the crown. But it's wrong. There is a crown too little. How can a thing like that be ignored? He talked for a long time about the matter; was very dissatisfied with me. And variations of that incident would be repeated in every shop, in every restaurant, in front of every beggar.[24]

IV

We must ask, finally, what relationship Kafka's writing bears to other writing of his time, and whether *The Castle* is representative of a genre, or whether it is an oddity and a phenomenon.

Expressionism is the word commonly used to describe the more advanced and experimental literature produced at the time Kafka was writing. Though there is controversy over its origins and even its meanings, most critics would agree that the term applies to a mode of writing that was at its height late in the first quarter of the present century and was characterized by a certain flamboyant rebelliousness (manifested both politically and artistically), and by an outpouring of expression that resulted from the fervency with which the writers sought utterance for urgently felt causes, or for subjective and spiritual states. Frequently in expressionistic images we find a violent yoking of disparates, as in the poetry of Gottfried Benn, or, in English, that of Pound and Eliot, while in the diction and syntax we see a short-circuiting, a series of veritable explosions of language, intended obviously to jolt, and showing little tolerance of conventional grammatical decorums. Though the substance of what was written was as varied as the authors were numerous, we may venture the generalization that the theme frequently deals with the murder of a father, symbolizing the upsetting of one old order or another. This parricidal convention was influential beyond the borders of Germany, has been commented upon by writers such as Stephen Spender and Goronwy Rees, and is amusingly parodied by Richard Hughes in his recent novel, *The Fox in the Attic*.[25]

[24] Brod, *Biography*, pp. 227–28.
[25] (New York, 1961), p. 124.

The extent to which Kafka participated in such a movement is not, however, easy to discover. Walter Sokel points out rightly that, through his friendship with Max Brod, and because of his connections with Kurt Wolff, who was instrumental in publishing the work of many Expressionists, Kafka is to be associated with that movement too.[26] Thematically too, and technically, in his manner of externalizing, projecting, and objectifying psychic or spiritual states, Kafka shares something with the Expressionists.[27]

Where Kafka differs from many of his contemporaries is in the realism of his surface and the lucidity of his style. Kafka's prose is crystalline. The descriptions, with their individual images, wind on and on in long, sinuous, qualifying, self-negating, subjunctive sentences. We perceive the everyday world through the fallible eyes of the protagonist, and scarcely question the individual statements, the ordinary landmarks enroute; and yet, when we arrive, we know little specifically and vaguely sense a threat, an enormous shadow over all. In his sharply descriptive, delineative technique it may be that Kafka shows the strong Naturalistic heritage which Wilhelm Emrich has convincingly claimed for him, noting his allegiance to Darwinism, and to other systems entailing an empirical, nineteenth-century world view. Speaking of Kafka's combination of precision and specificity, combined with an enveloping portentousness, Emrich writes, "The world he describes remains in the long run incomprehensible and strange to the describer himself. The summary enumeration of all existence does not lead, in the end, to a revelation of its meaning or its laws. . . . The sum total of all things that are known is, itself, incomprehensible." [28] For this reason, the protagonist, in this case K., one of the most resolute of all Kafka's major characters, is frustrated, deceived, and destined to spend himself, notwithstanding his firm intent and the solidity of his goal. Solidity and actuality have, for Kafka, no necessary relation. To illustrate with an aphorism of his own: "The crows declare that one single crow can destroy Heaven. That undoubtedly is true, though it does not prove anything against

[26] *An Anthology of German Expressionist Drama: A Prelude to the Absurd* (New York: Anchor Books, 1963), p. xi.

[27] There are excellent scholarly studies of Kafka's relationship to Expressionism, such as the early article by R. H. Thomas, "Franz Kafka and the Religious Aspect of Expressionism," *German Life and Letters,* II (October, 1937), 42–49.

[28] *Franz Kafka* (Bonn: Athenäum Verlag, 1958), pp. 31–34, and p. 421, note 26. Unfortunately this book has not been translated.

Heaven, since Heaven means precisely this: the impossibility of crows." [29]

It must be added, too, that Kafka himself did not feel very comfortable with the productions of his Expressionistic contemporaries. We learn from Gustav Janouch that on seeing a volume of poems by the Expressionist, Johannes Becher, Kafka declared that they were noise and hodgepodge, that he did not understand them, and that they were an outcry—nothing more. Similarly with respect to the drawings of Oskar Kokoschka: Kafka said he did not understand them, and that, to him, they signified merely profound confusion and turmoil in the painter.[30] In fact, advocacy of subordination to authority as a sign of true freedom is a theme not uncongenial to Kafka,[31] and his hospitality to such a view should make us cautious about linking him facilely with any ism, or with contemporaries who might have as their primary purpose shocking, startling, or throwing off the traces of an older way of life or art.

V

Curious, paradoxical, enigmatic, short-lived, and in a measure unclassifiable as he may be, Franz Kafka—not fifty years dead—has struck such a sensitive chord in those thousands who have studied, written, and commented on his work that today there are two large, book-size bibliographies listing the writings about him. In selecting from such a vast body of material, I have made it my purpose to exhibit as far as possible the diversity of interpretation with respect to one work. That the Castle represents salvation, and that K.'s effort is an effort to attain it, is perhaps the oldest of many theories, and derives from Brod's original postscript to the first edition. This interpretation was furthered and widely propagated by Edwin Muir, who in the introduction to his translation (1930) called *The Castle* a "religious allegory," to be compared to the *Pilgrim's Progress*. [Muir's essay introduces this collection.) From such an interpretation it is a

[29] Erich Heller has interpreted this aphorism profoundly as paralleling Kafka's own exorcising attempt in the writing of *The Castle*. Brod refers to the same saying in *Verzweiflung und Erlösung im Werk Franz Kafkas* (Frankfurt am Main: S. Fischer Verlag, 1959), p. 7.

[30] Janouch, *Gespräche*, pp. 52, 59.

[31] Janouch, *Gespräche*, pp. 78–79.

very long way to Charles Neider's psychoanalytical reading (p. 40 or to the view of Frederick Olafson (p. 83), who sees the book as a drama of moral consciousness standing alone, unencumbered, vulnerable, and true to itself. At the opposite end of the spectrum from Brod's view stands Erich Heller's eloquent interpretation. For Heller the Castle is neither Heaven nor Salvation—far from it! "*The Castle* is as much a religious allegory as a photographic likeness of the devil could be said to be an allegory of Evil. . . . *The Castle* . . . is a terminus of soul and mind, a *non plus ultra* of existence." The quest of K. becomes, like the paradoxical coexistence of Heaven and crows, the contradiction of its own success.

Franz Kafka is a phenomenon. He was a diffident writer. He was a reluctant writer. Not one of his major works is complete, and all that there was, he wished destroyed. Nor had he welcomed the publication of his earlier work. *Contemplation* (1912), had to be coaxed from him, and he weeded out so much that finally the limited edition of 800 copies had to be set in gigantic letters so that the contents could fill the ninety-nine page book. Despite all this, Kafka's effect in our time, and on today's critics, has been mesmeric. Somewhere he touched a nerve. What nerve, and how he touched it, is the subject of literally thousands of essays, of which the following are representative.

PART ONE

Interpretations

Introductory Note to *The Castle*

by Edwin Muir

Franz Kafka's name, so far as I can discover is almost unknown to English readers. As he is considered by several of the best German critics to have been perhaps the most interesting writer of his generation, and as he is in some ways a strange and disconcerting genius, it has been suggested that a short introductory note should be provided for this book, the first of his to be translated into English.

Kafka died in 1925 of consumption at the early age of forty-two.[1] During his lifetime he published only a few volumes of short stories and novelettes, all of them characterised by extreme perfection of form, and most of them wrung out of him by the persuasion of his life-long friend, Herr Max Brod, the well-known novelist. Before he died he destroyed a great number of the manuscripts he had been engaged on, but he left, among other things, including a number of aphorisms on religion, three long unfinished novels, *America, The Trial* and *The Castle*. He left explicit instructions as well, however, that these, along with all his other papers, should be burnt. As his executor, Herr Brod was in a very difficult position. In a note appended to *The Trial* he has given in full Kafka's dying instructions, and set out with the utmost candour his reasons for not following them. These reasons are entirely honourable, and his decision to publish the three novels has been approved by every responsible critic in the German-speaking countries. The novels themselves, however, provide the best data for judging the wisdom of a choice so difficult; for they are the

"Introductory Note" by Edwin Muir. From The Castle *by Franz Kafka. Translated by Willa and Edwin Muir. Copyright 1930 by Alfred A. Knopf, Inc. and renewed 1958. Reprinted by permission of Alfred A. Knopf, Inc. and Martin Secker & Warburg, Ltd. [This was the first edition of* The Castle *to appear in the English language*—ED.]

[1] In fact, Kafka died in 1924—ED.

most important of Kafka's writings, and two of them are masterpieces of a unique kind.

Herr Brod's courtesy has provided me with a few particulars about Kafka's life. He was born in Prague in 1883 of well-to-do Jewish parents, studied law at the university there, and after receiving his doctorate took up a post in an accident insurance office. After a love affair, which ended disastrously, he fell ill, symptoms of consumption appeared, and for some time he lived in sanatoriums, in the Tyrol and the Carpathians, but finally left them for lodgings in a village in the Erzgebirge near Karlsbad, which was to become the original of the village in the present book. Having partially regained his health, he went to live in the suburb of Berlin with a young girl who seems to have made him happy. Unfortunately the years of inflation came, food was scarce and bad, and he finally succumbed and was sent to a sanatorium near Vienna, where he died. Those last years before the collapse were the happiest of his life. The three unfinished novels which he left are an imaginative record of an earlier phase.

Of these novels two, *The Trial* and *The Castle,* are in a sense complementary, as Herr Brod points out at the end of this book. Both may be best defined perhaps as metaphysical or theological novels. Their subject-matter, in other words, is not the life and manners of any locality or country; it is rather human life wherever it is touched by the powers which all religions have acknowledged, by divine law and divine grace. Perhaps the best way to approach *The Castle* is to regard it as a sort of modern *Pilgrim's Progress,* with the reservation, however, that the "progress" of the pilgrim here will remain in question all the time, and will be itself the chief, the essential problem. *The Castle* is, like the *Pilgrim's Progress,* a religious allegory; the desire of the hero in both cases to work out his salvation; and to do so (in both cases again) it is necessary that certain moves should be gone through, and gone through without a single hitch.[2] But there the resemblance ends. For Christian knows from the beginning what the necessary moves are, and K., the hero of *The Castle,* has to discover every one of them for himself, and has no final assurance that

[2] [With all due respect to the meritorious translation of Edwin Muir, it must be said that he introduced both the major and the minor Kafka problems to this country. The major problem arose from his insistence that Kafka, a modern and more complex John Bunyan, wrote religious allegory . . .

From "The Minor Kafka Problem" by Meno Spann, *The Germanic Review,* XXXII (October, 1957), 165. Copyright ©. Reprinted by permission of the publisher, Columbia University Press.]

even then he has discovered the right ones. Thus while Bunyan's hero has a clear goal before his eyes, and a well-beaten if somewhat difficult road to it, the hero of this book has literally almost nothing. Kafka does agree with Bunyan in two things: that the goal and the road indubitably exist, and that the necessity to find them is urgent. His hero's journey, however, is a much more difficult business; for people's reports, ancient legends, one's own intuitions, even the road signs, may all be equally untrustworthy. If anyone wanted to estimate how immensely more difficult it is for a religious genius to see his way in an age of scepticism than in an age of faith, a comparison of the *Pilgrim's Progress* with *The Castle* might give him a fair measure of it. Yet hardly a fair measure, perhaps. For Bunyan's mind was primitive compared with the best minds of his age, and Kafka's is more subtly sceptical than the most sceptical of our own. Its scepticism, however, is grounded on a final faith, and this is what must make his novels paradoxical, perhaps even incomprehensible, to some contemporary readers. His scepticism is not an attitude or a habit; it is a weapon for testing his faith and his doubt alike, and for discarding from them what is inessential.

Accordingly in the present book and *The Trial* the postulates he begins with are the barest possible; they are roughly those: that there is a right way of life, and that the discovery of it depends on one's attitude to powers which are almost unknown. What he sets out to do is to find out something about those powers, and the astonishing thing is that he appears to succeed. While following the adventures of his heroes we seem to be discovering—almost without being fully aware of it—various things about those entities which we had never divined before, and could never perhaps have divined by ourselves. We are led in through circle after circle of a newly found spiritual domain, where everything is strange and yet real, and where we recognise objects without being able to give them a name. The virtue of a good allegory is that it expresses in its own created forms something more exact than any interpretation of it could. The *Pilgrim's Progress* did this in its very circumscribed way; it is more exact in detail than any theoretical exposition of it could be; but indeed its interpretation, a banally simplified theological system, existed full-blown before it. Having admitted this, one may see better the extreme difficulty of Kafka's attempt. For his allegory is not a mere recapitulation or recreation; it does not run on lines already laid down; it is a pushing forward of the mind into unknown places; and so the things he describes seem to be actual new creations which had never existed before. They are like palpable additions to the intellectual world, and ones which cannot be comprehended at a single glance, for there is meaning behind meaning, form behind form, in them all.

I have indicated less than a tithe of the things which may be found in this book and in *The Trial,* and that is all that I can do here, for Kafka's writings have an almost endless wealth of meaning. His superb gifts as a story-teller, and his genius for construction, hardly need to be pointed out; it is obvious, however, that without them he would have been unable to introduce us to his strange world. In a recent issue of the *Literarische Welt* Herr Willy Haas remarks very finely of him that he has a tremendous power of deducing the real from the real, of starting from something concrete and sinking his thought into something which seems still more concrete. This is his method, and in the present novel with its consummate construction, few of those links between the concrete and the more concrete are left out; the progress of the invention coincides with the exploring and creating thought, so that in being carried forward by the action we are at the same time participators in the discovery and spectators of a world being built.

The unique quality of Kafka's temperament is shown in his attitude to this world which he is investigating. That attitude may be best described by negatives. He avoided scrupulously the pose of the spectacular wrestler with God, which even certain great writers, such as Baudelaire and Rimbaud, have incomprehensibly assumed, but from which he was saved by the modesty of his view of his own place in the universe, and by his sense of humour. He avoided also the gesture of resignation, for what meaning could resignation have—except a pragmatic one—in face of the things he was investigating? Nor did he take refuge in irony, though certain episodes in his novels are saturated with it. Perhaps his temper is shown best in two axioms of his: that compared with the divine law, however unjust it may sometimes appear, all human effort, even at its highest, is in the wrong; and that at all times, whatever we may think, the demand of the divine law for unconditional reverence and unconditional obedience is beyond question. But—here again he surprises us—unconditional reverence and obedience do not seem in his eyes to have excluded the strictest scrutiny, or even the most acute comic observation. His descriptions of the Heavenly Powers are very curious. He notes their qualities and their foibles with something of the respectful appreciation of Plutarch writing of Alexander or Cato. To more ignorant eyes, it is true, those foibles might appear mere faults, but to him, as to Plutarch in somewhat analogous circumstances, they are worthy of esteem as the qualities of superior beings, qualities perhaps disconcerting and even incomprehensible to the writer himself, but qualities nevertheless which would be found to incarnate unquestionable virtues were his mind capable of understanding them. In Kafka's descriptions of the conflict of his heroes with heavenly destiny there are, amid all the bewilderment and nightmare apprehension, interludes of the purest humour.

Of Kafka's style one can get an adequate idea only by going to the original. It is a style of the utmost exactitude, the utmost flexibility, the utmost naturalness, and of an inevitable propriety. His vocabulary is small, but his mastery of it is absolute. By means of the simplest words he can evoke new effects and convey the most difficult thoughts. His management of the sentence is consummate. Flowing without ever being monotonous, his long sentences achieve an endless variety of inflection by two things alone, an inevitable skill in the disposition of the clauses, and of the words making them up. I can think of no other writer who can secure so much force and meaning as Kafka does by the mathematically correct placing of a word. Yet in all his books he probably never placed a word unnaturally or even conspicuously. His sentences are constructed so easily and yet balanced so exactly that, even when they are very long, he hardly ever needs the support of a semicolon, the comma doing all that is required. For the comma, indeed, with its greater flexibility, he shows a partiality; or he loves the sinuous line, the sentence which flows forward, flows back on itself and flows forward again before it winds to its determined end. His dialogue is untranslatable. It is not the realistic dialogue of which almost all contemporary novels are full; it is a separate form of art with its own laws. In sense of style there is no living English writer who approaches it, except Mr. Joyce in certain pages of *Ulysses*.

"The Castle of Despair"

by Henri Daniel-Rops

Franz Kafka is one of the most astounding examples (together with Proust, and, in another way, Joyce) of an artist who creates his work out of that which essentially destroys both the artist and the work. It is not an exaggeration to say that in our age a great many works of art are no more than the records of these acts of destruction. Kafka was rooted deeply enough in the human drama, and his art in its formidable lucidity was great enough to fashion a portrait, a likeness, of this being so irretrievably shattered. A Kafka goes infinitely further in this direction than a Proust whose meaning remains almost exclusively psychological, or a Joyce who tried to explain everything in terms of myths and verbal magic. By the very anguish that engulfed him, an anguish metaphysical in the true sense of the word, Kafka was one of the truest and most dramatic witnesses of modern man and his struggle with nothingness.

The Castle is without question Kafka's most important book. Important, first, because of its length, which is so unusual in its author; his shorter works might lead one to think that one of the main elements of their perfection lay in their brevity; it is now clear that this highly personal art can adapt itself to the difficulties of plot development, and far from wearying the attention of the reader constantly spurs it on. This book is unfinished, but, in a sense, neither more nor less so than all of Kafka's works, which we know he regarded as provisional and incomplete. It is unimportant that the adventure of the Land Surveyor intent on making contact with the Castle should have a few extra scenes. It is not by the succession of episodes that Kafka commands and holds our attention; we might even say that

---

Henri Daniel-Rops, "The Castle of Despair," trans. Muriel Kittel, in The Kafka Problem, *ed. Angel Flores (New York: Octagon Books, Inc., 1963), pp. 184–91. "The Castle of Despair" by Henri Daniel-Rops, trans. by Muriel Kittel. From* The Kafka Problem, *ed. Angel Flores (New York: Octagon Books, Inc., 1963), pp. 184–91. Reprinted by permission of Angel Flores.*

from the moment we enter his world everything (including ourselves) finds itself set in a strange fixity, wherein doubtless lies the profound explanation of the amazing metaphysical tension that prevails there.

But the importance of *The Castle* depends less on these purely exterior conditions than on the internal elements we find there which are fully significant to Kafkan art and thought. Of all Kafka's books this is the one which best realizes what seems to have been his most unerring aim: to achieve the mysterious, the secret, the esoteric without yielding to the fantastic. From this standpoint the book is purer (in the sense that we speak of pure poetry or of matter being chemically pure) than the majority of his works.

In "The Metamorphosis" there was an arbitrary hypothesis: that a man could be changed into a monstrous cockroach; in *The Castle* there is nothing like that; the plot is completely banal. The myth springs from nothing. It has no need of startling phenomena. It is natural and at the same time charged with terrible significance. It could be said that the deepest mystery is obtained by pushing realism to extremes. All the details are simple and commonplace; yet the writer subjects them to a transmutation which makes them seem to compete with each other in enveloping us with some weighty secret. Nowhere in his work has Kafka been so close to that ideal he set for his art: "dazzled blindness before the truth."

In *The Castle* we recognize the two dominant themes of Kafkan thought, both used with extraordinary persuasive force. The actual plot behind these two hundred and fifty pages of writing can be reduced to very little: It is concerned merely with a man's efforts to make contact with an inaccessible castle and its inhabitants. This castle, which may have been suggested to the author's imagination by the Rhadschin at Prague, is defined in a contradictory way. Depending on the point of view, it is "only a wretched-looking town, a huddle of village houses"; or else "a place of renown and certainties; its bell when it rings proclaims the accomplishment of those things the heart dimly longs for." It is evidently, then, the symbol of those inaccessible realities toward which man gropes without ever being able to reach. For in the character of K. the author is concerned with man in general; the very name used to describe him is significant—the Land Surveyor—the man who measures everything.

Through this outline, then, appear the two fundamental themes found throughout Kafka's work. One is concerned with a suprahuman justice, strictly incomprehensible, even absurd, that condemns a human being to think of himself as always—to use the excellent expression of Groethuysen—"indicted though free." Carried to less extreme than in *The Trial,* this theme is nonetheless sustained from the beginning to the end of *The Castle* with a whole paraphernalia of trials, judgments to give and verdicts to accept. It is perhaps even given a new direction here: one episode (where Sordini would like to make a person do evil in order to attain the good) seems to indicate that Kafka, following Kierkegaard, admitted the complete incompatibility of this suprahuman justice with human morality. The surveyor may work in vain, he will not *deserve* to be introduced to the castle. This entrance is a gift, an act of grace; let only those to whom the powers that be grant their favors for nothing aspire to it.

And it is the certainty of the futility of all effort that makes Kafka's view of man's position so depressing. This is the second essential theme in his work: that of an entirely unacceptable state which is nonetheless completely accepted. The incomprehensible events that weave the hours of this life mysteriously shorten the days, reverse the times of rest and work, continually upset logic, are indeed only symptoms of this intolerable situation in which everyone endures life nevertheless. Many writers today take for their theme the impossibility of modern man's resolving the antagonism between conscience and external forces. Malraux's *Man's Fate* is one such testimony. But literary work usually springs from the actual impact between man and the obstacle he beats himself against. Kafka, in my estimation, is the only one who has placed his work not at the point of conflict itself, but beyond, right in the forbidden zone. He does not seek to resolve the contradiction, he accepts it. His work actually thrives on it. He writes, in spite of appearances, more the novel of inaccessible forces that ignore man than the novel of man seeking to conquer them.

Such an art, which tries with such superhuman force to grasp the intangible, meets with a basic difficulty, the difficulty of the mystics, the difficulty that Rimbaud faced: how to make comprehensible to men of flesh and blood that which by its very nature goes beyond life. For Kafka's symbols are not formulated, nor are they even the most important thing. Actually he becomes more and more wary of symbols. But the more we uncover his thought the more we desire to understand the meaning of the symbolism, surmising that it corresponds to something irreplaceable in our consciousness. But at the same time the symbol recedes and we are unable to grasp it completely. The law, finding the law, yet never being able completely to understand the law. Kafka's world is a universe of absurdity through which the human intelligence is groping, and in the end can lead only to despair. Art which should elucidate this despair is only the most futile of interpreters since it can end in nothing but uncertainties. The endless search for certainties in life as in death only led Franz Kafka to the brink of nothingness. It is as a perfectly natural conclusion to this "spiritual quest" (as Rimbaud would have said) that his order to destroy all his works must be understood. Such an art may seem to *us* to borrow grandeur from the force that is really destroying it; to the artist it is only a failure by comparison with what he wanted to accomplish.

Nevertheless we must not consider the aesthetic side alone if we are to understand what it is in this literature of Kafka that causes us (we must admit) such a surprising uneasiness. It is not only because he takes us into a fourth dimension that he fascinates us. We have the feeling that he touches us in a part of our being where we like to keep our secret connivances. This Prague Jew, nourished on the Talmud, haunted by the search for and despair of the law, later deeply influenced by the philosophy of the famous Dane, Sören Kierkegaard, gives us, should we say, one of the most moving and most apt symbols of modern man at the mercy of God and at the same time ignorant of Him. Let us see how.

His entire work is dominated by the theme of judgment, sentence and acquittal. In Franz Kafka's universe every man has to undergo judgment and is liable to punishment because of the simple fact that he lives and must die. But can we at least make this judgment favorable to us? Is acquittal possible?

Kafka's despair replies in *The Trial:*

> The Judges of the lowest grade haven't the power to grant a final acquittal, that power is reserved for the highest Court of all, which is quite inaccessible to you, to me, and to all of us. What the prospects are up there we do not know and, I may say in passing, do not even want to know. The great privilege, then, of absolving from guilt our Judges do not possess, but they do have the right to take the burden of the charge off your shoulders. That is to say, when you are acquitted in this fashion the charge is lifted from your shoulders for the time being, but it continues to hover above you and can, as soon as an order comes from on high, be laid upon you again . . . In definitive acquittal the documents relating to the case are completely annulled, they simply vanish from sight, not only the charge but also the records of the case and even the

acquittal are destroyed, everything is destroyed. That's not the case with ostensible acquittal. The documents remain as they were, except that the affidavit is added to them and a record of the acquittal and the grounds for granting it. The whole dossier continues to circulate . . . A detached observer might sometimes fancy that the whole case had been forgotten, the documents lost, and the acquittal made absolute. No one really acquainted with the Court could think such a thing. No document is ever lost, the Court never forgets anything.

Such then is man's fate which none can escape. Each one of us is imprisoned in himself, subject to a responsibility which he may pretend to forget, but which others, Another, will not forget for him. And so over the whole of Kafka's universe hangs an atmosphere of horror, related to the one we are familiar with in a Rimbaud, a Strindberg, a Novalis, a Hölderlin, and also in painters like Civetta, Breughel the Elder, Van der Goes, Hïeronymus Bosch, and in some pictures of Dürer.[1] Actually others have had a clear vision of this unremitting captivity of mankind. Where Kafka is more original is in the reply he gives to this dramatic questioning.

Some people have tried to reply to this question by a denial: deny man's fate, go beyond it. This is what the surrealists have done, following Rimbaud and Lautréamont (but by infinitely more rudimentary methods). To escape mankind or reality is a way of evading oneself. Since the pressure of a soulless world has weighed more heavily on modern man a large number of these attempts at evasion have appeared in our literature, some of them rather over-simplified. There is nothing of that in Kafka. This man dominated by a passion for the absolute is really a spiritual son of Kierkegaard who accepts man's fate even to the limit of his worst agony, and from his suffering draws the basic element of his greatness.

At the same time nothing could be more mistaken, as some interpreters have suggested, than to regard Franz Kafka as a sort of lucid madman who would extract from his madness a magnificent orchestration, a kind of a crystalline symbolism. If this were so then the only rational people would be those who go through life without bothering to look for a meaning, and who, without knowing it, are imprisoned in the revolting hard skin of their routines and complicities like the grotesque cockroach of "The Metamorphosis." No, Kafka was not mad; but his enquiries took place in a region where men are usually

[1] Picabia, among our contemporaries, is in this line.

not willing to enter, doubtless out of fear they might find themselves there for good.

To understand the judgment we need to know the law. But can one know the law? Kafka answers this question in each of his books, we might even say in the least of his fragments. He replies in the negative. Whether he speaks to us of the Castle, the symbol of inaccessible realities which man in spite of all his efforts can never reach; whether he analyses the emptiness of all knowledge in "Investigations of a Dog," the reply will always be the same. Man does not know the law, he is incapable of understanding the word. He will beat himself against his own reflection and against the mirror that shows it to him. He is a prisoner; if he sees clearly, like the hero in "The Metamorphosis," he suffers more on that account, but conscious of it or not, he is always imprisoned. On the other hand if he wishes to try to escape from himself, this can only be done by the premeditated destruction of all that makes his existence real—like the terrifying protagonist of "The Burrow," a horrible creature, a kind of mole, who decides to leave the earth of mankind and bury himself in a deep burrow, living there no longer like a being really alive but like a grub, in a series of petty routines, minor details, and a whole disgusting collection of bestial habits.

Kafka's conclusion is that man is a prisoner who cannot escape his fate. He is so acutely conscious of it that his life is to a certain extent inhibited by it. This fatalism is expressed very well in "The Next Village." It is precisely this fatalism that he accepts. Since there is no way out, and since the mind cannot even penetrate the meaning of this ridiculous balance of forces that holds us prisoner, there is nothing to do but to yield, to bow the head and be resigned to it.

> Don't be so obstinate; we must admit that there is no defence against this justice. So admit it at the first occasion, it is only later that you will be able to try to escape from yourself, only afterwards; and even then you will only succeed if someone comes to your help.

Be reconciled then; but to whom?

It is impossible not to respond to the mysterious sort of appeal which re-echoes in the numerous phrases analogous to those we have just read. Beyond doubt there is in Franz Kafka a sense of waiting—the waiting for a mediator, for an infinite, superhuman power who can give men the answers to the dread questions of life. It could be described as an almost sacramental waiting. The man of Kafka's world is "indicted though free." It is an intolerable condition. He aspires to a judgment, to a formulated law that would allow him to know exactly where he stands. Kafka's characters are in a way *beyond good and evil* because for them everything is reduced to an attempt at clairvoyance that does not allow them to put the problem in the way it should be put. Judgment, that is, the affirmation of good and evil, is a respite, the most sensitive of respites. Beyond a certain boundary there is evil, there is the abyss, the night without end and the existence without peace.

In this world, entirely dominated by the highest themes proposed to man, what is there lacking that keeps one from feeling completely held by it? Upon reflection, it seems to me to lack a sense of responsibility. It is a world of absurdity, and we can only think of it as such. But if we can accept without understanding the *how,* we have an instinctive need to know the *why.* This man always threatened by punishment, and whose efforts are always futile, is like a vapid reflection of the Christians' sinner. But the religious teaching of good and evil, of sin and forgiveness gives a deeper meaning to life. Kierkegaard, Pascal, starting from similar observations, sink roots much deeper into the mystery of existence. We might say that Kafka's world bears witness to that "wretchedness of man without God" or rather "without the possibility of grace." But even so man is still quite laden with promises—with even more promises than Kafka believed possible. And Max Brod was right when he wrote of his friend in the novel [*The Kingdom of Love*] in which he affectionately recalls him: "His writing brings to men who wander through the night the presentiment of higher and irreplaceable good toward which they are groping. . . ."

K. of *The Castle:* Ostensible Land-Surveyor

by Erwin R. Steinberg

Most critics seem to take at its face value K.'s statement at the beginning of *The Castle* that he is a land-surveyor hired by the Count. Ronald Gray, for example, says, "K. at once affects, on his arrival at the inn, to have no inkling of the castle's presence, though it soon becomes obvious that he has come because of a summons from the owner of the castle himself." [1]

Tauber does indicate at first that K. is not what he seems: "K. pretends that he has been appointed by the Castle as Land Surveyor. . . ." [2] But he never examines the implications of that pretense, and immediately after his announcement of it writes as though K.'s claim was valid. A few lines later, for example, he calls K. "The Land Surveyor" (p. 133). And a few pages later he indicates that he considers that at least after K. arrives he has a valid appointment—although it "is valid only in an equivocal way, so that the appointed man is at the same time not appointed" (p. 136). And he goes on to speak of "the history of his appointment" and the "acts of carelessness [which] played a part in his appointment" (p. 136).

Whether K. is in fact what he claims to be is an important point which should be examined carefully. For if K.'s seeking to be accepted by the Castle is symbolic of man's seeking salvation, questioning the validity of K.'s credentials and thus his right to press his claim on the Castle raises the parallel question of man's right to salvation.

An examination of *The Castle* indicates that there is little evidence to support K.'s claim either that he is a land-surveyor or that he was hired by the Castle. And there is a good bit of evidence to the contrary.

---

[1] *Kafka's Castle* (Cambridge, Eng., 1965), p. 27.

[2] Herbert Tauber, *Franz Kafka* (London, 1948), p. 132.

Let us look first at the opening scene in which he makes his claim. Questioned about his presence, K. replies:

> "What village is this I have wandered into? Is there a castle here?"
>
> "Most certainly," replied the young man slowly, while here and there a head was shaken over K.'s remark, "the castle of my lord the Count Westwest." [3]

K. admits that he *wandered into* the village. He obviously does not know where he is. There is nothing about the statement that suggests a purposeful visit. Nor is there anything to suggest, as Gray says, that "K. . . . affects to have no inkling of the castle's presence." The only reason to question the honesty of K.'s indication that he knows nothing about a castle lies in his claim made immediately after, that he has been hired by the Count. But as we shall see, that claim itself is highly questionable.

Pressed by the ill-mannered Schwarzer, K. strikes back:

> "Enough of this fooling," said K. in a markedly quiet voice, laying himself down again and pulling up the blanket. "You're going a little too far, my good fellow, and I'll have something to say tomorrow about your conduct. . . . Let me tell you that I am the Land-Surveyor whom the Count is expecting. My assistants are coming on tomorrow in a carriage with the apparatus. . . . That it was too late to present myself at the Castle I knew very well before you saw fit to inform me. That is why I have made shift with this bed for the night, where, to put it mildly, you have had the discourtesy to disturb me. That is all I have to say. Good night, gentlemen." And K. turned over on his side toward the stove. (p. 5)

Schwarzer's call to the Castle brings a quick denial of K.'s claim. But almost immediately a call from the Castle brings a reversal of that denial. K.'s claim, it would seem, is genuine (p. 7).

Later, however, we are warned against trusting any message that comes from the Castle over the phone. In talking with K., the mayor says:

> When anybody calls up the Castle from here, the instruments in all the subordinate departments ring, or rather they would all ring if practically all the departments—I know for a certainty—didn't leave their receivers off. Now and then, however, a fatigued official may feel the need of a little distraction, especially in the evenings and at night, and may hang the receiver up. Then we get an answer, but an answer of course

[3] Franz Kafka, *The Castle* (definitive edition), (New York, 1959), p. 4.

> that's merely a practical joke. And that's very understandable too. For who would take the responsibility of interrupting, in the middle of the night, the extremely important work up there that goes on furiously the whole time, with a message about his own little private troubles? I can't understand how even a stranger can imagine that when he calls up Sortini, for example, it's really Sortini that answers. Far more probably it's a little copying clerk from an entirely different department. On the other hand, it may certainly happen once in a blue moon that when one calls up the little copying clerk Sortini himself will answer. Then, indeed, the best thing is to fly from the telephone before the first sound comes through. (p. 94)

In the light of such a statement, the curious reversal of the Castle's original denial of K.'s claim becomes highly suspicious.

Furthermore, K.'s reaction to the Castle's acceptance of his claim raises doubts:

> K. pricked up his ears. So the Castle had recognized him as the Land-Surveyor. That was unpropitious for him, on the one hand, for it meant that the Castle was well informed about him, had estimated all the probable chances, and was taking up the challenge with a smile. On the other hand, however, it was quite propitious, for if his interpretation was right they had underestimated his strength, and he would have more freedom of action than he had dared to hope. And if they expected to cow him by their lofty superiority in recognizing him as Land-Surveyor, they were mistaken; it made his skin prickle a little, that was all. (pp. 7–8)

If K. really is a land-surveyor hired by the Castle, why is it "unpropitious for him" that the Castle had recognized him? What can the statement of the Castle's "taking up the challenge with a smile" mean other than that K.'s claim is a false one and that he is being dared to prove it? If he really is the land-surveyor, why should he take the Castle's recognition of him as a sign that the Castle was trying "to cow him"?

The matter of the Assistants is further evidence against K.'s claim. According to K.'s original statement, they are due the next day with his apparatus (p. 5). The next day, two men who purport to be his assistants do appear!

> Not until he was up with the landlord, who greeted him humbly, did he notice two men, one on either side of the doorway. . . . it was the men he had already met, who were called Arthur and Jeremiah. . . . "Who are you?" he asked, looking from one to the other. "Your assist-

> ants," they answered. . . . "What?" said K.; "are you my old assistants, whom I told to follow me and whom I am expecting?" They answered in the affirmative. "That's good," observed K. after a short pause; "I'm glad you've come. Well," he said after another pause, "you've come very late; you're very slack." "It was a long way to come," said one of them. "A long way?" repeated K.; "but I met you just now coming from the Castle." "Yes," said they without further explanation. "Where is the apparatus?" asked K. "We haven't any," said they. "The apparatus I gave you?" said K. "We haven't any," they reiterated. "Oh, you are fine fellows!" said K.; "do you know anything about surveying?" "No," said they. "But if you are my old assistants you must know something about it," said K. They made no reply. "Well, come in," said K., pushing them before him into the house. (pp. 23–24)

It is obvious from the passage that Arthur and Jeremiah are not K.'s assistants. Later evidence proves them to have been sent by the Castle (p. 302).

The scene also suggests that K. is not expecting assistants. For surely if he is he would not take Arthur and Jeremiah. For if he does, when his own assistants appear, how could he explain to the already suspicious villagers his acceptance of the two from the Castle? Surely a surveyor can be expected to know his own assistants. The obvious answer is that the statement about assistants is as untrue as the statement that K. is a land-surveyor.

There is other evidence of the same kind throughout the book. A curious letter arrives acknowledging that K. has been "engaged for the Count's service" (p. 30). But it says nothing about surveying; and as K. himself notices, it uses terms which suggest a much lesser status:

> There was of course a danger, and that was sufficiently emphasized in the letter, even elaborated with a certain satisfaction, as if it were unavoidable. That was sinking to the workman's level—"service," "superior," "work," "terms of employment," "responsible," "workers,"—the letter fairly reeked of it, and even though more personal messages were included, they were written from the standpoint of an employer. (p. 32)

The summary of K.'s thoughts about the letter denies K.'s original claim of having been invited to the village by the Count:

> Nor did the letter pass over the fact that if it should come to a struggle, K. had had the hardihood to make the first advances; it was very subtly indicated and only to be sensed by an uneasy conscience—an uneasy conscience, not a bad one. It lay in the three words "as you know,"

> referring to his engagement in the Count's service. K. had reported his arrival, and only after that, as the letter pointed out, had he known that he was engaged. (p. 33)

Later, the Mayor indicates that the village has no need of a surveyor (p. 77). And when the landlady charges K. with having lied about his claim ("You're not telling the truth. Why don't you tell the truth?"), he does not press his claim or become indignant at the charge. He simply replies, "You don't tell the truth either" (p. 411).

The clearest evidence, however, that K.'s claim of having been hired by the Castle as the land-surveyor is false comes in the fourteenth chapter, where a summary of K.'s thoughts indicates very clearly that he came to the village "as a wandering stranger" who expected to leave the next day, or perhaps a day or two later at the most in the unlikely event that he found some work:

> Because of Schwarzer the full attention of the authorities had been most unreasonably directed to K. at the very first hour of his arrival, while he was still a complete stranger in the village, without a single acquaintance or an alternative shelter; overtired with walking as he was and quite helpless on his sack of straw, he had been at the mercy of any official action. One night later might have made all the difference, things might have gone quietly and been only half noticed. At any rate nobody would have known anything about him or have had any suspicions, there would have been no hesitation in accepting him at least for one day as a stray wanderer, his handiness and trustworthiness would have been recognized and spoken of in the neighborhood, and probably he would soon have found accommodation somewhere as a servant. Of course the authorities would have found him out. But there would have been a big difference between having the Central Bureau, or whoever was on the telephone, disturbed on his account in the middle of the night by an insistent though ostensibly humble request for an immediate decision, made, too, by Schwarzer, who was probably not in the best odor up there, and a quiet visit by K. to the Mayor on the next day during official hours to report himself in proper form as a wandering stranger who had already found quarters in a respectable house, and who would probably be leaving the place tomorrow unless the unlikely were to happen and he found some work in the village, only for a day or two, of course, since he did not mean to stay longer. (p. 216)

Certainly these are not the thoughts of a man who had been invited to the village by the local authorities to serve as its surveyor.

The Publisher's introductory Note to the definitive edition of the novel (and, as indicated, in earlier editions the Editor's Note) carries a warning that K.'s claim is not to be trusted:

> As *The Castle* remains unfinished, however, the following paragraph from the Editor's Note to the first American edition should be preserved: "Kafka never wrote his concluding chapter. But he told me about it once when I asked him how the novel was to end. The ostensible Land-Surveyor was to find partial satisfaction at least. He was not to relax in his struggle, but was to die worn out by it. Round his deathbed the villagers were to assemble, and from the Castle itself the word was to come that though K.'s legal claim to live in the village was not valid, yet, taking certain auxiliary circumstances into account, he was to be permitted to live and work there." (p. vi)

The important point is not that the Castle branded K.'s legal claim "not valid," but rather that Max Brod—and perhaps even Kafka himself—referred to K. as the "*ostensible* Land-Surveyor." If the adjective could be proven to have been Kafka's, the case against K.'s claim could be declared, perhaps, a little stronger. It rests securely enough, however, on the textual evidence given above.

This demonstration of the lack of validity to K.'s claim adds an additional dimension to the usual interpretation of *The Castle*. Critics generally interpret the novel as the story of man's attempt to reach salvation, religious, or otherwise. Thomas Mann, for example, in his introductory "Homage" to the novel describes "K.'s relations with the 'Castle,' or rather [his attempt] to set up relations with it [as an attempt] to attain nearer, in other words, to God and to a state of grace" (p. xiv). Tauber understands the novel to mean that: "The striving after justice, after the unequivocal word is in vain. But it is also not publicly refuted, because in it a basis of truth is effective: man's being coordinate with a spiritual certainty, with a real significance of his personal existence with God." (pp. 183–84). Camus speaks of K.'s "attempt . . . to recapture God [and] to try to enter . . . the desert of divine grace." [4]

It is one thing, however, for a man—or Man—to seek a salvation to which he feels he has some right. In many religions, for example, the possibility of that right is explicit: it may either be given by election or earned by prayer, acts of penitence, or good works. In *The Castle,* if K. is indeed a land-surveyor and if he has indeed been hired

[4] Albert Camus, "Hope and the Absurd in the Work of Franz Kafka," in *The Myth of Sisyphus* (New York, 1960), p. 99.

by the Count, he has some reason (or right) to expect to get through to the Castle, to communicate with the Count or his emissaries. And symbolically, if a man—or Man—has been chosen or has earned consideration from God, he has a reason (or a right) to expect salvation.

But how if, as I have attempted to show above, K.'s claim is false? Then he is making demands he has no right to make. He is seeking a salvation he has neither been awarded nor has earned.

If this is the picture that Kafka is giving us, then to the previous interpretation of *The Castle* we must add an additional ironic twist. Not only does K. pursue doggedly a salvation he cannot hope to achieve (or, if one credits Brod's story about the conclusion Kafka planned for the novel, he receives too late—p. vi). He seeks a salvation which he has not been promised, which he has not earned, and to which he has no reason to feel he has a right. If this is Kafka's picture of Man's journey through life or of his relation to God, it is even more bitter than critics in the past have led us to believe. Not only will Man not achieve salvation. He is presumptuous in even seeking it.

K. as Impostor: His Quest for Meaning

by Walter Sokel

Whereas the hunger artist makes his fraud explicit, the immense deception perpetrated by the Land Surveyor K. in *The Castle* is never stated explicitly, and K. has, therefore, fooled most readers, critics, and exegetes of the novel. K. claims to have been called and appointed land surveyor by the castle which controls the village into which he has strayed one night. He makes us believe that the castle authorities, by refusing to honor his claim, treat him unjustly and deprive him of what by right is his. He presses his claim with such urgency and consistency that the reader feels compelled to accept it at face value and to see in K. a victim of soulless bureaucracy or to construct elaborate schemes of interpretation based on the "injustice" done to K. Consequently, *The Castle* appeared in critical literature as a satire on bureaucracy, an adumbration of totalitarianism, an allegory of social injustice or of the religious problem of man's insistence on justice and God's grace. All these interpretations are the result of the critics' being duped by K.'s colossal fraud. A close reading of the text reveals that K. has no legitimate claim on the Castle because he never was appointed land surveyor. This truth of the novel is revealed by inconsistencies in the plot and by a brief passage of K.'s inner monologue. These allow only one conclusion: K. had never been called by the Castle.

K. has no document to prove his call. He promises, however, that his assistants will soon arrive with his apparatus. They never come. Instead K. is given two new "assistants" by the Castle. These assistants know nothing about land surveying and have no apparatus. K. has

---

"K. as Impostor: His Quest for Meaning" (editor's title), from Walter Sokel, Franz Kafka *(New York: Columbia University Press, 1966), pp. 39–44.*

never seen them before. Thus the "proof" of K.'s appointment, which the promised arrival of his old assistants and apparatus was supposed to be, never materializes. The fact that K. accepts his new assistants without waiting for his old assistants or ever thinking of them shows that, in all likelihood, they do not exist.

A telephone inquiry at the Castle produces the answer that nothing is known of K.'s appointment. Immediately thereafter, a call from the Castle reverses this first answer and confirms K.'s claim. K.'s mental reaction to this information unmasks him as an imposter. Instead of registering with simple satisfaction the news that the "misunderstanding" has been cleared up, K. considers the Castle's recognition of his claim "unpropitious." He takes it to be a "smiling acceptance" of his "challenge," designed to "cow him" by "lofty superiority." The term "challenge," used by K. in this context, shows that he does not expect to step into a promised position but that he comes with the purpose of fighting the Castle and forcing it to yield something to him, either the coveted office or something else. It is clear that he was never appointed land surveyor and called to the Castle. He is a stranger who, for reasons which we shall examine, "challenges" the Castle to submit to his unfounded claim. The Castle seems to "accept" his "challenge" and plays a game with him which forms the plot of the novel.

This close reading of the text alters the whole basis of interpretation of Kafka's last and greatest novel. It can no longer be maintained that the conflict between justice and injustice, no matter on what level, is its theme. Its theme is rather K.'s attempt to make everyone, including the reader, believe that justice is the problem and that the injustice inflicted upon him is his motive in his struggle with the Castle. Kafka has K. conduct his campaign so skillfully and emphatically that he persuades most readers to believe him, contrary to the textual evidence he himself provides. In his richest and most profound work Kafka depicts the victory of fiction over reality. The deception perpetrated by his character triumphs not over the other characters—for no one in the novel really believes K.—but over the reader.

Kafka achieves this amazing triumph of art by the masterful application of a narrative perspective which misleads the reader into mistaking the protagonist's view for the truth. However, while creating this victory of fiction, Kafka at the same time exposes its falseness through his protagonist's own oblique self-revelations. Furthermore, the fact that the hero's claim never attains true recognition in the novel shows its vanity. In a letter to Max Brod, written in the year

1922, at the time of *The Castle*'s composition, Kafka defined the writer's essence as "vanity." Kafka's late work, especially his artist stories, "A Hunger Artist" and "Josephine," shows vanity both as narcissism and as futility. It shows that the attempt of subjectivity to impose its terms upon external reality must always fail.

The Castle answers K.'s attack with an ironically exact retribution. It meets his unreal claim by an equally unreal appointment. Klamm's letter appoints K. as Land Surveyor, and he will henceforth be addressed as such; but he obtains no land to survey and is never established in an appropriate office. The title given him by the Castle is as gratuitous and empty as his pretended call. The Castle gives him assistants who are irrelevant to his professed profession. They can assist him in his land surveying as little as can the instruments he claims he has but is unable to produce. These assistants also cause him to do to them what he claims the Castle has done to him. As the Castle locks him out and will not admit him, he locks out his assistants and refuses to let them come to him. K. himself displays the cruelty and injustice he ascribes to the Castle. Moreover, even as he took his mistress away from Klamm, his own chief, so he loses her again to one of his assistants. In this late work judgment appears not as destruction, but as ironic retribution.

The Castle counters K.'s maneuver by presenting a universe in which there is no certainty and nothing is what it seems to be. This is the necessary consequence of the fact that the protagonist, too, is not what he seems to be. That is, K.'s self is not a fact but a pretense. It is a desperate experiment, an attempt to impose his fiction upon the reality that confronts and excludes him. He needs this fiction to break into and become part of the reality he faces.

Kafka, in *The Castle,* describes the fundamental situation of modern man, for whom neither the world nor his own self is given and certain. Like every man, K., in order to be, has to be recognized and related as an individual to the whole of society; he must have a specific calling. In order to get his call, he must already be someone, an accredited and required expert. However, K. knows he has no call and is, therefore, nothing. He is a stranger, utterly unconnected, and superfluous—locked out by the *Schloss* functioning in its basic meaning of "lock." Since a human being cannot live permanently outside humanity, K. desperately needs to enter it, that is, to become someone needed and recognized. In order to live, he has to "unlock" the lock with which humanity excludes him. As the dominant necessity of life and the essence of desirability, *"das Schloss"* presents to him its other meaning in the guise of the magically beckoning and unattainable castle. It is K.'s staggering and superhuman task to create the call he needs. He has to pretend that he already possesses what he has come to get—the necessary prerequisite for beginning an integrated and authentic existence. Therefore, his battle with the Castle is not a whim but a desperate necessity. Precisely because he has no objectively valid claim for recognition, he must force the Castle to honor his subjective pretense—his fiction—as the truth. K. fights to become in truth what he pretends he is—the land surveyor called by the Castle.

K.'s quest is a metaphoric statement of the lifelong struggle which Kafka's entire writing sought to describe. (Significantly, his first work bears the title "Description of a Struggle.") At the time he composed *The Castle* Kafka wrote to his woman friend and lover, Milena, that he was given nothing, that he must create not only his present and his future but his past as well. His task is, therefore, infinitely more difficult than that of other men. For not only must he fight the battle for his future that every man has to wage but, while engaged in that battle, he must also be acquiring a past, a ground on which he can stand and all others can take for granted as their birthright and inheritance.

Kafka related this peculiar predicament to the fate of the Westernized Jew in Europe who, already uprooted and cut off from his ancestral traditions, is not yet permitted to enter fully and truly the life of his hosts. Beyond this personal and national meaning, however, Kafka presents in *The Castle* the task facing modern man in general. Unmoored from his spiritual and social anchorage, expelled from his once secure place in the cosmos, modern man, as the Existentialists point out, has to make his own identity and project his own existence instead of assuming it as given. Kafka's fragmentary novel depicts the tragic irony and ultimate impossibility of this enterprise.

K. and the Quest for God in Life

by Herbert Tauber

In the conception of surrender, Kafka's peculiar symbol for the relationship with God corresponds to the representation of faith in those women-figures of Dostoevsky's, who take upon themselves the lowest abasement in dumb devotion. In Sonja Semenovna in *Crime and Punishment,* who is compelled by fate to earn bread for her dependents by being a prostitute, and yet remains devoted to God and humble before Him, this surrender in faith is reduced to an extreme formula. That she endures the vileness thrust upon her by fate and does not go to her death, but goes on living in the consciousness of her sin, is her loyalty to God. Even if this motif of sexual surrender in Dostoevsky is very different in the whole range of its interpretation from Kafka's use of it, in that for the women in the village it represents an ennobling and not an abasement, yet a common background of emotion is at work in it. As Amalia's attitude shows, for Kafka, too, it is a question of finding the extreme expression for the surrender in the relationship with God. The fundamental attitudes of surrender and revolt that comprehend the relationship with God and the world are bundled together in the same way into a formula in the relationship between the women and the officials. What Sonja experiences as the demand of immediate fate, confronts Amalia as the demand made by Sortini, the Castle official. That is to say, it has already been reduced to the formula, "How can God allow such things?" At the same time it embraces the possibility of Amalia's happiness (Frieda and the landlady find their highest happiness in their relationships with the offi-

---

"K. and the Quest for God in Life" (editor's title), from Franz Kafka: An Interpretation of his Works *by Herbert Tauber, trans. by G. Humphreys Roberts and Roger Senhouse (New Haven: Yale University Press; London: Martin Secker & Warburg, Ltd., 1948), pp. 143–46. Copyright 1941 by Dr. Oprecht & Helbling A. G., Zürich. Reprinted by permission of Martin Secker & Warburg, Ltd.*

cials; Olga says, "There are no unhappy love affairs with the officials.") —the possibility of a humble relationship with God, in which all fate is accepted as a trial. The distress of abasement and the happiness of acceptance—the relationship with the world and the relationship with God—are reduced in the relationship with the officials to a common denominator. Within the framework of the whole novel this symbolism appears as the result of a forceful concentration. In this case, Kierkegaard's saying "All burrowing into existence consists in establishing connections" [1]—is aimed at in the most extreme way—as is also the case with Dostoevsky.

In Dostoevsky's Sonja the extreme case of being exposed to the inextricable world is conjoined with the most intimate concealment in God. The world as "challenger" is not so immediately co-ordinated with God in his case as in Kafka's. The mystery of evil, of the devil, prevents this connection. Ivan Karamazov, on the other hand, fulfils this reflex connection and in his case there results, too, that which is produced in Amalia's case directly through the official's proposal, revolt.

The surrender, the saying "yes," confronts not only something God expects of man, but grace at the same time: the possibility that is afforded man of saying "yes," the loving entry into existence, the personal relationship with God. That is why for the landlady the relationship with Klamm is the highest happiness and not to be compared with any other earthly fulfilment. The possibility of this comprehensive relationship with God is, for man, set about with the finite, a surpassal of himself, seen from without, a kind of presumption. The landlady therefore says the description "Klamm's mistress" is a wild exaggeration, but then, it is true, she herself lays claim to it as an "Upgrading that cannot be lost." Olga's laughing at Frieda during K.'s first visit to the *Herrenhof* points to the incompatibility of this relationship for the low figure of man. It is Frieda's greatness that she accepts this risk of being laughed at, that she takes humbly upon herself this incompatibility. It must be admitted that this incompatibility is also, the other way round, oppressive for man. The possibility of a relationship with God makes him feel his being set about with the earthly as almost unbearable suffering, and lends his existence the character of a constant desperate and unsuccessful struggle to live up

[1] Eng. Kierkegaard's *Concluding Unscientific Postscript to the Philosophical Fragments* (Copenhagen, 1846), trans. David F. Swenson, O.U.P., 1941. German: *Abschliessencle unwissenschaftl* (Jena, 1910).

to this relationship with God in eternity. K. believes he sees this in Frieda, too. When he listens to her voice, he seems to hear "in her tone . . . against her will, an echo, rather of countless disappointments than of past triumphs."

K.'s strivings in the village are devoted to getting beyond the incompatibility between the village and the Castle, to living in finite existence and at the same time towards God in a true way. He wants to detach the relationship with God from its hidden inwardness and to make the individual acts of life correspond to it. He would like to see his express appointment fulfilled in a finite sense, too, and not merely "allowed" under the accidental conditions of an outward, impalpable fate.

His affair with Frieda is at the same time a relationship with this hidden inwardness. Frieda, the barmaid at the *Herrenhof,* is the mistress of the official, Klamm, who is also K.'s invisible and unapproachable superior. At his first visit to the *Herrenhof* K. wins her love. He spends a night with her in the taproom in passionate self-oblivion. They roll over on the floor in each other's embrace—hard by the door of Klamm's room. In the morning Frieda gives up her post, and follows K. to his inn. In Frieda the secrets of the relationship with God seem to open up before K. She has a look of "special superiority."

The promise of femininity appears in her with a special significance. It is the motherly surrender and loyalty to being that are fulfilled in womanliness, and through them the dreamed-of nearness to the forces of fate that stand over and nourish man, which awakes in K. the hope of contact with the ultimate basis of existence. A parallel situation can be found in *The Trial,* where there is expressed, in K.'s foiled attempt to win the Court attendant's wife, a striving after a practical proof of manliness and self-glorification over against an opponent, from whom the woman is to be snatched away; but here the Land Surveyor's original intention is, in his becoming one with the girl, to let the powers of love which touch the divine and intensify and deepen the whole inner being serve the advantage of his struggle for the depths of his own existence, for his connection with the divine foundation. Of course, in this case, it is not a question of the demonstration of a dubious self-glorification as in the scene in *The Trial,* but of deeper needs.

But K. falls victim to his delusion. His belief, that everything earthly lives immediately in the direction of God and has its outlet in Him, is met by the experience of the constant concealment of Klamm. Instead of the expected unity, which is expressed in K.'s belief that through Frieda's agency "an almost corporal connection with Klamm, close enough for widespread understanding, has arisen," his connection with the girl causes only confusion. The possibility of striving, of battle, of self-assertion in the claim to clarity of the relationship with God, is abandoned by him in the very first union of the lovers in a surrender in which the vile and the disgusting—the filth and the puddles of beer in which the embraces take place—are forgotten and accepted. This union of the lovers, in which deepest delight and disgust, deepest self-discovery and self-abandonment are indissolubly united, is really a marriage with this earthly side, in its immensity, ambiguity, in its meaningless fulfilments and its failure in the question of the ultimate wishes of the human heart. The claim to be raised above this questionable sphere is shown to be thrown away through this complete abandonment to the sensual.

In this self-oblivion there is simultaneously expressed, all the same, a true fundamental feeling towards existence: the loving surrender to that which has no foundation and is unfathomable. That is why K., through his affair with Frieda, comes into the warm stream of circulation of the protecting and serving forces of life; whereas without them he would be "a null, staggering, behind will-o'-the-wisps gleaming like silk, like that worn by Barnabas or that girl from the Castle." His hopes, of an immediate step forward from this situation to Klamm and into the Castle, prove to be delusion all the same, because life, although it always points beyond itself, offers only itself in its transitory figures and fulfilments. In K.'s relationship with Frieda the full satisfaction with the circle of spiritual inwardness and the urge to outward clarity of realization stand thus opposed to one another.

The Castle: A Psychoanalytical Interpretation

by Charles Neider

The discovery of a key to Kafka's novels was made only gradually. My interest in Kafka's dream technique led me to investigate the literature of dream dynamics. I was soon forced to conclude that Kafka had applied Freud's dream findings deliberately. Not only that: he had utilized the core of psychoanalytic knowledge as the basis of his allegorical myths. In addition, he had infused his works with autobiographical details. One recalls Kafka's secretiveness, and his sly remark that there was a secret cabala in his work.

* * *

I hope to prove that *The Castle* contains a cohesive and deliberate pattern of symbols and a cryptic meaning whose existence is indubitable and that it is no longer permissible to argue vaguely concerning its meaning.

My findings are fourfold:

1. *The Castle* contains a web of symbols that are mainly sexual in nature—those symbols common to dreams, folklore, and the unconscious as discussed by the psychoanalytic movement, especially by Freud, Jung, and Stekel.

2. It is a literary panorama of the states of consciousness as discovered by the psychoanalytic movement.

3. It presents in detail the dynamics of the Oedipus complex.

4. It contains a web of nomenclatural symbolism.

The influence of psychoanalysis on Kafka is hardly surprising. By 1912, when Kafka "broke through" artistically, the psychoanalytic

---

"The Castle: *A Psychoanalytical Interpretation" (editor's title), from Charles Neider,* The Frozen Sea *(New York: Oxford University Press, 1948), p. vii; pp. 122–29. Reprinted by permission of the author.*

movement was in full swing, exploring the mythological, anthropological, and artistic ramifications of its discoveries. Freud and Kafka were produced by identical cultural factors: both were Jews, both were born in Central Europe (Freud in Moravia, now, like Bohemia, part of Czechoslovakia), both struggled against the shibboleths of the Gentile Austro-Hungarian Empire; both were irregular, both were skeptical, both were intent on discovering the reality and through it the possibility of human amelioration.

In peopling the depth psychology Kafka mirrored his own culture. He made bureaucrats out of the gentlemen of the unconscious and hypersensitive moralists, resembling philistines, of his preconscious characters. He visualized the unconscious as the great authority, with feudal powers. His choice of the castle as the chief symbol of the novel was by no means accidental. The fact that he did not select a religious symbol (such as cathedral or chapel) to represent woman, mother, and the unconscious is indicative of his non-religious position.

Kafka's symbols and hidden meanings manipulate the reader's unconscious. They are part of a hypnotic program. One comprehends him, realizes him, without necessarily understanding him. His cool style effectively disguises his potions. Reading him, one moves close to the unconscious. That is why we are disturbed, why we wish to resist. His symbols and meanings are interconnected. They possess a fluid significance, on many levels, some contradictory. The problem of the individual *vs.* authority is also the problem of the son *vs.* the father and the conscious *vs.* the unconscious. On the social level the villagers' belief in the existence and power of the castle is superstitious; on the psychological it is based on reality, the dominance of the unknown unconscious. In one context K. is a hero battling irrational authority and demanding "inalienable" rights and a brand of justice based on reason and logic. In another he is sick and blind, seeking to find and enjoy the very things that in the previous context he wishes to destroy.

The Castle is a modern myth in which man's tragedy is his fruitless quest for his unconscious and for the resolution of his neurotic torment there. K. is a mixture of Oedipus and Hamlet. He is doomed merely to seek to do the very things that Oedipus with a brash hand did. He is denied the pleasure of possessing Jocasta and the cosmic penance of tearing out his eyes. He is doomed to be an Oedipus just short of realization, with the eternal failure of a Sisyphus.

SYMBOLISM

There are two types of symbolism in The Castle: *mythical symbolism*[1] *and symbolic action.*

MYTHICAL SYMBOLISM

A castle, like a village, town, citadel, and fortress, is a symbol of woman and mother. A count is a father symbol, like emperor, king, and president.[2] The count's permission is necessary for K. to enter the castle; i.e. the father's permission is necessary for the son to possess his mother incestuously. Land too is a symbol of woman and mother, as indicated by the expression "mother earth." A land surveyor is therefore one who measures the mother—the incestuous implication is obvious. K.'s surveying apparatus, an obvious symbol of his masculinity, never arrives; i.e. he is not adequate sexually, although he has unusual sexual drives. K. telephones the castle (the old-fashioned telephone is a male symbol) and later discovers that there is no real connection with the castle. The lack of sexual connection is an important theme of the novel.

When K. embarks on his first village walk he pauses near the church (♀), a chapel (♀) with barnlike (♀) additions. He flings a snowball at a window (♀); a door (♀) opens, a plank (♂) is shoved out to rescue him from the snow. He enters the house of the tanner Lasemann (probably from the German *lass,* weak, since the tanner is described as weary and weak). Filled with steam, it is the scene of washing and splashing (water symbolizes birth or rebirth), with children loudly crying and with a woman nursing an infant at her breast. Coitus is performed symbolically by two men bathing in a wooden tub (♀) "as wide as two beds." The men stamp and roll (rhythmic and violent acts symbolize coitus). The children, trying to draw close, are frustrated by "mighty splashes of water"—i.e. social taboo. One of the men, with his mouth hanging open (♀), showers drops of warm water on K.'s

[1] I have applied this term to those dream symbols which psychoanalysis has described as archetypal and phylogenetic. While it is true that mythical symbols may be found in any fictional work, in Kafka's work they are overwhelmingly predominant. It is not true that all objects fall into the categories of male and female symbols and that therefore Kafka's symbols are accidentals.

[2] The symbol of Venus (♀) and the symbol of Mars (♂) will henceforth be used to denote female and male symbols respectively.

face. "From a large opening (♀), the only one in the back wall, a pale snowy light came in, apparently from the courtyard, and gave a gleam as of silk (♀) to the dress of a woman . . . almost reclining in a high arm-chair." Emphasis on materials is a constant motif, since materials (from *mater,* mother) is a female symbol.

K. dozes and awakes refreshed. He "poked with his stick (♂) here and there" and "noted that he was physically the biggest man in the room." His courage rises when he approaches female symbols. " 'I say,' cried K. suddenly—they were already near the church (♀), the inn (♀) was not far off, and K. felt he could risk something—'I'm surprised that you have the nerve to drive me round on your own responsibility; are you allowed to do that?' " Again Gerstäcker's mouth falls open, displaying "a few isolated teeth" (♂). K.'s assistants have black pointed beards (♂) and tight-fitting clothes. (Their clothes resemble uniforms and uniforms symbolize nudity.) K.'s coitus with Frieda is preceded by many sexual symbols: the uniforms of the Herrenhof peasants, the peephole (♀) through which K. sees Klamm, Klamm himself, Frieda's "low-cut cream-colored blouse," the leather bag (♀) hanging at her girdle, from which she draws the small piece of wood to stop up the peephole (wood is a female symbol used here as a male symbol because of its shape), the peasant dance around Olga, Frieda's whip (♂), et cetera.

At the superintendent's K. witnesses a mass of symbols: the superintendent's gouty leg (♂), the candles (♂), cabinet (♀), shed (♀), chest (♀), the rolls (♂) of paper (♂) documents (paper is derived from papyrus, a long-stemmed plant with a spray on top). The Bridge Inn landlady has retained three (♂)[3] keepsakes from Klamm, who sent for her three (♂) times. In the schoolroom there are gymnastic apparatus (♂), wood (♀), shed (♀), sausage (♂), stove (♀), candle (♂), and cat (♀).

The celebration of the Fire Brigade festival is a phallic fest, the fire engine symbolizing the phallus. The male symbolism is powerful. The celebration occurred about three (♂) years ago, on the third (♂) of July, and Amalia's father was third (♂) in command of the brigade. Sortini leaped over the engine shaft (♂) to approach Amalia. Trumpets (♂) are prominent. Amalia's letter from Sortini is the third (♂) and last delivered during the novel's progress, K. having received two others from Klamm. Amalia is the third (♂) woman whom we see in

[3] According to psychoanalysis, the sacred number three is a mythical symbol of the whole male genitalia.

a sexual relation to the castle officials, the Bridge Inn landlady and Frieda being the other two. Female symbols are also present, in particular the necklace of garnets (♀) which the Bridge Inn landlady gave Olga and which Olga gave to Amalia. Coming from a former mistress of Klamm, the necklace was an important gift, a symbol of fertility. Olga impulsively conferred it on her sister because she unconsciously understood Amalia's personal tragedy and hoped by the gift to make her normal.

The Herrenhof landlady is obsessed with the idea of clothes. Kafka emphasizes the material (♀) of her dresses. K. comes to a secret agreement with Pepi. He will knock three (♂) times for admittance.

SYMBOLIC ACTION

An interesting paragraph concerns K.'s memory of having climbed a wall in his boyhood. He recalls a church (♀) partly surrounded by a high wall (♂) in the market place of his native town.

> Very few boys had managed to climb that wall, and for some time K., too, had failed. It was not curiosity which had urged them on. The graveyard had been no mystery to them. They had often entered it through a small wicket-gate, it was only the smooth high wall that they wanted to conquer. But one morning—the empty, quiet market-place had been flooded with sunshine, when had K. ever seen it like that either before or since?—he had succeeded in climbing it with astonishing ease; at a place where he had already slipped down many a time he had clambered with a small flag between his teeth right to the top at the first attempt.

Climbing symbolizes coitus. The failure of the boys may have resulted from the unwillingness of their partners or from various psychic or physical causes. The episode alludes to K.'s first sexual success, which was unexpectedly easy after much difficulty. Its memory succors him while he is dragged on the arm of Barnabas through the snowy night. Barnabas takes him to his house, not to the castle—i.e. to domesticity rather than incest. But K. regards the castle as his true home, since that is where his "parents" reside. He ponders: "So it was only Barnabas who was at home, not he himself."

The incident of Klamm's sledge (♀) symbolizes an act of onanism.

> He opened the wide door (♀) and could without more ado have drawn a flask (♀) out of the side pocket (♀) which was fastened to the inside of the door; but now that it was open he felt an impulse which he could not withstand to go inside the sledge; all he wanted was to sit there for

> a minute. He slipped inside. The warmth . . . was extraordinary . . . although the door, which K. did not dare to close, was wide open . . . one could turn and stretch on every side, and always one sank into softness and warmth.

K. is stupefied by this womblike warmth. Finally he reaches into the pocket of the closed door (the forbidden one) and pulls out a flask. The brandy is like a perfume, sweet and caressing. "Can this be brandy?" he asks himself doubtfully. "Yes, strangely enough it was brandy, and burned and warmed him. How wonderfully it was transformed in drinking out of something which seemed hardly more than a sweet perfume into a drink fit for a coachman!" But now he is regretful. " 'Can it be?' K. asked himself as if self-reproachfully, and took another sip."

Suddenly the electric lights (of his conscience) blaze on and he is caught in the act by Momus, a father surrogate. "This is unheard of," says Momus, pushing his hat (♂) back on his forehead. K. retrieves his cap (♂) from the sledge and notices "with discomfort" that the brandy is dripping from the footboard. K. refuses to accompany Momus and Momus "ran the tip of his tongue round his slightly-parted lips," a sexual gesture. Momus orders the horses stabled, i.e. the passions locked up. He and the coachman disappear. Finally the electric lights go off. Then it seems to K. that "these people" have broken off all relations with him. He had "won a freedom such as hardly anybody else had ever succeeded in winning." Yet he feels that there is nothing more senseless and hopeless than this freedom. This is perhaps a reference to the "freedom of the artist" on which Kafka insisted in his relations with F.B., and which he finally found to be utterly sterile if divorced from the main stream of existence.

He wrenches himself free of this "freedom" and returns to the Herrenhof. There he meets Gardena, Momus, and Pepi. A brandy he orders from Pepi he finds undrinkable. He desires more of the Klamm-brandy, which is sweet, but Pepi, as if frowning on onanism, curtly says she has no other kind.

The Messengers: Barnabas and Amalia

by Heinz Politzer

On the evening of the fourth day K. sends Barnabas to the Castle in order to request a personal interview with Klamm. Whatever he does or says during the next day is colored by his expectation of the messenger's return. High hopes and grave doubts alternate in his mind. Barnabas, by delivering favorable messages, has lived up to his name, which, according to the Acts of the Apostles (4:36), means "son of consolation." [1] On the other hand, these messages, K.'s "decree of appointment," and his laudatory citation as a Land-Surveyor, have also turned out to be malicious specimens of Klamm's peculiar sense of humor in spite of the comfort they offered. There are other reasons for distrusting Barnabas. He had introduced himself with words of evangelical simplicity: "Barnabas is my name. . . . A messenger am I," and K. could not help noticing the noble quality of his clothes: "He was dressed all in white; not in silk, of course, . . . but the material he was wearing had the softness and dignity of silk" (29).[2] Yet as soon as he follows Barnabas to his hut, he is disillusioned. He recognizes that "he had been bewitched by Barnabas' close-fitting, silken-gleaming jacket, which, now that it was unbuttoned, . . . displayed a coarse, dirty gray shirt patched all over, and beneath it the huge muscular chest of a farm-laborer" (40). Furthermore, this messenger who looks like a peasant turns out to be a journeyman in the service of Brunswick, the cobbler, and it seems as if he would let this menial work interfere with the errands he undertakes at the behest of

[1] Herbert Tauber, *Franz Kafka* (New Haven: Yale University Press, 1948), 170 n.

[2] [Although the numbers without letters refer to the American edition of *The Castle* (1954), there are, in fact, some minor textual differences between the American and British editions—Ed.]

K. Barnabas is a cobbler's son and resembles a cobbler much more than a messenger (in Austrian usage the word *Schuster* ["cobbler"] has the connotation of "misfit"); nor does the garment which has drawn K.'s attention by any means represent the livery of an official Castle servant; it was sewn for him by his sister, Amalia (226). Only a certain duplicity of behavior identifies him as an envoy of Klamm, whose ambiguity seems to have influenced the servant: Barnabas hurries about when carrying out the orders of the Castle but drags his feet when he is supposed to deliver K.'s answer. The Land-Surveyor cannot be blamed for bursting out, "It is very bad for me to have only a messenger like you for important affairs" (157).

It turns out, however, that this ambiguity is inherent only in Barnabas' function as an emissary from the Castle and does not extend to him as a person. When Olga, his second sister, initiates K. into the story of her family, the Land-Surveyor discovers that the messenger's personal intentions toward him are thoroughly honorable. "He did not sleep all night because you were displeased with him yesterday evening," Olga informs K. (229). It is not his fault when the part he plays as Klamm's errand boy arouses K.'s suspicions. The Castle bears the blame, for it makes use of his services without having acknowledged him as its servant. Thus Barnabas finds himself in essentially the same predicament as K. and yet what seems to be an ordeal to the Land-Surveyor is at the same time the fulfillment of the most tender hopes of the messenger and his family. K.'s arrival appears to them as the turning point after three years of misery. Klamm's letters, questionable as they are, have meant to them "the first signs of grace" (296). Barnabas himself is more than willing to serve on sufferance without any right. He is happy like a little boy, "in spite of all the doubts that he had about his capability." "He confined these doubts to himself and me," Olga reveals, "but he felt it a point of honor to look like a real messenger." Nor should K. deny him his sympathy, since it is also his point of honor to be a "real" Land-Surveyor.

In spite of his doubtful appearance Barnabas is really a messenger of hope. The hope he offers is a human hope. When K. hears about Barnabas' true feelings, he has an opportunity to realize that his mere presence is able to raise the spirits of others and to comfort them by supporting their expectations. To see this, he has only to desist from mirroring himself in them and to accept them for what they are, just as he demands to be accepted himself. After Barnabas was entrusted with his first letter, Olga informs K. he "laid his head on my shoulder, and cried for several minutes. He was again the little boy he used to be." K.'s response to her tale, though it was fraught with emotion, is cold: "All of you have made pretences" (295). He dismisses as mere fabrication the messenger's outbreak of joy and does not want to have any part of it.

Although K. is groping desperately for help, he refuses to give it to others. When Olga greets him almost jubilantly, "How fortunate that you have come!" he simply turns away, annoyed at such a display of enthusiasm: "He had not come to bring good fortune to anyone. . . . Nobody should greet him as a bearer of good tidings; whoever did this, was liable to confuse his ways, claiming him for causes for which he was at nobody's disposal under such coercion; with the best of intentions he had to refuse." [3] He is afraid of confusing his ways by being a messenger of good tidings himself. Yet the path before him is already so tortuous that he need not fear to confuse it still further by a simple human response. On the contrary, any kindliness he showed to others might help him along his way. This is one of the passages in *The Castle* where K. actually could have changed his course. But it is no accident that Kafka deleted these sentences in his manuscript; they would have pointed too clearly in a direction neither he nor his hero was prepared to take in their self-inflicted isolation.

Olga is as favorably inclined toward K. as her brother is. It was she who accompanied him on his first walk to the Herrenhof (42 f.). When she exposes the secret of her family to him in a long night's story, she wants to help him as much as to be helped by him. Her very name may be derived from the German equivalent of "holy." [4] There are striking similarities between their fates. Like him she hopes to establish "a certain connection with the Castle" (286) by making love with its subordinates. Before K. tumbled down to embrace Frieda on the taproom floor, he observed Olga in a mating dance with a number of villagers, and when he emerged, he saw her again, her clothes torn and her hair deranged (50, 55). At that time her debauchery had not particularly surprised him. He took it as a sign of simple sexual jealousy, a revenge for his having preferred Frieda to her. But now he learns that Olga's villagers were in actual fact servants of the Castle:

[3] From a deleted passage, published by Brod at the end of his postscript to the German edition of *Das Schloss*, p. 497.

[4] R. Gray, *Kafka's Castle* (Cambridge: Cambridge University Press, 1956), p. 119.

"For more than two years, at least twice a week, I have spent the night with them in the stable" (285). Olga's promiscuity differs from K.'s love-making in one decisive aspect: she does not surrender to the Castle in this indirect and unpromising way to further her own ends. She sacrifices herself to atone for Amalia.

Amalia's story is a novella in its own right, connected to the rest of the narrative by the remarks which K. makes about it. Since he mirrors himself in Amalia, he cannot perceive the true stature of this woman who towers over the village in silent grandeur. One feels that she is present throughout Olga's tale, although she exits from the scene before Olga begins. "She went without taking leave of K., as if she knew he would stay for a long time yet" (223). Unnoticed she slips away and reappears, loses herself again in the darkness of the hut, and yet she seems to dominate it with her personality even when she sleeps. Almost superhuman powers are noticeable in her who dared defy the Castle.

This, then, is Amalia's story: Three years ago, on the third of July, the village celebrated the dedication of an engine which the Castle had presented to the local Fire Brigade. The gift was accompanied by a number of trumpets, "extraordinary instruments on which with the smallest effort . . . one could produce the wildest blasts; to hear them was enough to make one think the Turks had come already" (247). These trumpets produce angelic and satanic sounds, as do the brass instruments used in the Oklahoma theatre in *Der Verschollene;* they indicate that a moment of great importance is at hand and prepare the reader for a meeting between the human and the more-than-human.

At this point, a point remote and vague in Olga's memory, the Castle and the village are united for the first and only time in the novel. Accordingly the season is summer, and on the scene the customary snow and fog are replaced by a green meadow and a murmuring brook. The whole gathering is devoted to a wholesome human purpose, the control of the demonic force of fire. On the other hand, the wild blasts of the trumpets evoke the image of polygamous Turks and these, in turn, the hordes of philandering Castle servants, who, one can surmise, are converging also on this lawn. Nor can one overlook the suggestively ambiguous central image, the fire engine, which is really a big water squirter (*Feuerspritze*).

Even a Castle representative is present, Sortini, who "is supposed to be partly occupied with fire problems." But the joyful occasion has not succeeded in breaking down the barriers traditionally existing between officials and villagers. Keeping close to the Castle's gift, the phallic fire engine, Sortini refuses to mingle with the crowd. Only when Barnabas' father, the third in command of the Fire Brigade, offers apologies to him (for what?), does Sortini react. He lets his eyes rest on Amalia, "to whom he had to look up, for she was much taller than he. At the sight of her he started and leaped over the shaft to get nearer to her; we misunderstood him at first and began to approach him . . . but he held us off with uplifted hand and then waved us away. That was all." It is not all, alas. For the one glance he exchanged with the girl seems to have impressed Amalia unduly. Her stunned silence ever after almost seems to justify a remark made by Brunswick, the cobbler, that "she had fallen head over ears in love" (248). The following morning she receives a letter, couched in most vulgar terms, ordering her to visit Sortini at once at the Herrenhof. The girl tears the letter to pieces and throws the shreds in the face of the messenger who has waited outside the window. This constitutes Amalia's sin (249).

The Castle, in its majestic impassivity, refrains from punishing Amalia in any overt way. But the villagers begin to withdraw from the girl as well as from her relatives. As if the daughter's guilt were by association also the father's, he loses first his honorary post with the Fire Brigade, then his customers. The family becomes anonymous; it is now named after Barnabas, the "least guilty" (273). Amid a community of primitive serfs, the Barnabas family lives in a ghetto assigned to pariahs by the slaves who are their neighbors. The only indication of the Castle's participation in the general ostracism of this family is the fact that it waited for the appearance of so lowly a creature as K. before it allowed Barnabas to go on his semiofficial errands on his behalf. The view of the parish serving the outcast would indeed be a prime specimen of the double-edged irony indulged in so brilliantly by Klamm and his colleagues.

Now we understand why Barnabas felt called upon to serve the Castle as a messenger; he wanted to atone for the insult inflicted upon Sortini's errand boy. By the same token Olga attempted to expiate Amalia's refusal of Sortini's embrace by becoming the prostitute of the Castle's subordinates. Her sacrifice fails. There is no indication of the official's reconciliation; but then neither he nor the Castle has ever given any indication of having taken offense. Olga comments bitterly,

"We had no sign of favor from the Castle in the past, so how could we notice the reverse now" (268)?

A further complication in the story is that it is impossible to establish with certainty the identity of the woman whom Sortini had summoned to the Herrenhof. The letter is addressed to "the girl with the garnet necklace" (249). This disastrous piece of jewelry had passed hands twice before it landed around Amalia's neck. The Bridge Inn landlady, the owner of the Bohemian garnets, had lent them to Olga, and Olga had decorated her sister with them, she did not know why (245). Sortini's summons, then, is directed at each of the three women who had been seen with the jewels at one time or another during this day: at Gardena, who had been Klamm's mistress but being no longer a "girl" was the least probable choice; at Olga, who certainly would have responded to the official's crude beckoning, since she is willing to surrender to the still cruder calls of the servants; and at Amalia, who actually wears the garnets when she is introduced to Sortini. She is the most unlikely to be singled out by Sortini, and this is the very reason why his letter descends upon her as one of those fatal lightning flashes which, bursting forth from indistinct heights, hit the target least expected to be their aim.

Sortini is as elusive as the Castle he represents. His function at the celebration is dubious; "perhaps he was only deputizing for someone else." He is described as "very retiring," and yet he is capable of savage aggression, as his letter shows. He is "small, frail, reflective looking," but backed up by the huge and loudly colored fire engine, he seems to fill the festive scene with his portentous presence. Although he is smaller than Amalia, even his upward look is condescending. Moreover, "one thing about him struck all the people who noticed him at all, his forehead was furrowed; all the furrows . . . were spread fanwise over his forehead, running to the root of his nose" (244). Imitating the ground plan of a labyrinth, these furrows attract the onlooker and lead him inevitably down to the level of Sortini's eyes, the eyes that have proved so fateful to Amalia.

A rather hectic discussion has developed as to the meaning of this official ever since Brod compared Sortini's letter to Kierkegaard's vision of Mount Moriah, where God asked Abraham to sacrifice his child. For Brod, Sortini's epistle represents "literally a parallel" to Kierkegaard's *Fear and Trembling*, "which starts from the fact that God required of Abraham what was really a crime . . . ; and which uses this paradox to establish triumphantly the conclusion that the categories of morality and religion are by no means identical."[5] Brod's attempt at coordinating God's claim on Isaac and Sortini's design on Amalia has prompted Heller to observe that it means,

> without any polemical exaggeration, to ascribe to the God of Abraham a personal interest in the boy Isaac, worthy rather of a Greek demi-god. Moreover, He, having tested Abraham's absolute obedience, did not accept the sacrifice. Yet Sortini . . . can, to judge by the example of his colleagues, be relied upon not to have summoned Amalia to his bedroom merely to tell her that one does not do such a thing.[6]

Emrich, on the other hand, sees in Sortini an allegory of the spirit per se: "Where spirit is nothing but spirit any more and appears as an isolated and abstract region, it is the very perversion of the human spirit."[7] In the final analysis Emrich is merely translating Brod's theological position into philosophical terms: what is good for the God of Abraham is also good for the spirit of pure abstraction. Heller's rebuttal is strong and sharp enough to puncture Emrich's thesis as well as Brod's. To visualize this Sortini as an absolute of any sort amounts to positing a paradox too paradoxical even for Kafka's wildest imagination. To answer the question raised by Sortini's letter, Kafka would have had to finish the novel and reveal the meaning of the Castle, the secret of which is shared by its officials. Hence we are not surprised to find the image of Sortini veiled by the same insoluble mystery which distinguished the Count Westwest, his master.

There is, however, an element of surprise in the Amalia episode. It offers us at least the hint of a turn to the better, which Kafka may have had in mind for his hero at one point or another. To grasp this hint we have to turn to the heroine rather than to her would-be seducer, Sortini. Amalia astonishes us indeed, and not only because of the space Kafka has devoted to her story. (The scene in her house covers approximately one-sixth of the book.) He granted his heroine what he denied his heroes: the ability to survive, and even transcend, despair.

Amalia is the only female in Kafka's gallery of women who does not conform with the observation he made in a letter to Brod, early in May 1921: "It is strange how little sharp-sightedness women possess; they only notice whether they please, then whether they arouse pity,

[5] Postscript to the German edition of *Das Schloss,* p. 488.

[6] Erich Heller, *The Disinherited Mind* (Cambridge: Bowes & Bowes, 1952), pp. 176–77, [and the Heller selection here following, pp. 77–78—Ed.]

[7] Wilhelm Emrich, *Franz Kafka* (Bonn: Athenäum, 1958), p. 363.

and finally, whether one is hankering for their compassion; this is all; come to think of it, it may even be enough, generally speaking" (*B*, 323).[8] Amalia is sharp-sighted, although in a very peculiar way. Like Olga she is a "great strapping wench" (41); and yet she is distinguished from her by her "cold, hard eye," which, K. remembers, frightened him when he saw her for the first time (267). To be sure, this does not indicate much more than K.'s inability to view himself in her as he is wont to do in the eyes of Frieda, Gardena, and even Olga. The narrator, more perceptive than his hero, confirms the hardness of Amalia's glance but also mentions its clarity. It was, he adds, "never leveled exactly on the object she was looking at, but in some disturbing way always a little past it, not from weakness, apparently, nor from embarrassment, nor from duplicity, but from a persistent and dominating desire for solitude." Even K. is both startled and spellbound by this look, "which in itself was not ugly but proud and sincere in its taciturnity." Thus he is moved to tell her, "I have never seen a country girl like you" (219). Here the narrator allows K. to articulate an insight more profound than he can consciously grasp. It seems that Kafka himself is subtly playing with his language here, demonstrating once more the inner unity of his imagery. Amalia is no country girl, no feminine version of the man from the country. She is no *Am-ha'aretz* like Joseph K. and K., the Land-Surveyor. She knows, for she has seen.

We shall have to assume that Amalia learned whatever she knows about the Castle from looking at Sortini. We are told precious little about her history before this meeting. She is the youngest member of the family and may have enjoyed the advantages which a family concedes to its youngest child. This is probably the reason why her mother has lent her every bit of her lace for the blouse she is to wear at the celebration, an injustice which induces Olga, the older one, to cry half the night. Both sisters have been looking forward to the occasion, but Amalia seems to be in a state of special expectation. Her father, with the one-track mind of a man, predicts, "Today, mark my words, Amalia will find a husband." Olga, on the other hand, notices her somber glance. "It has kept the same quality since that day, it was high over our heads and involuntarily one had almost literally to bow before her" (245). About the meeting with Sortini we have likewise only negative evidence: although we are told that the official looks up to her, the fact that she returns his glance is not mentioned. (As

[8] Kafka, *Briefe: 1902–1924* (Frankfort: Fischer, 1958).

can be seen from the silence with which Kafka enveloped K.'s transition from the bridge to the village, he refrains from spelling out decisive moments involving the total existence of his figures.) That Amalia's life has been changed here and now we can only guess from her behavior later on in the day: she is even more silent than usual and remains sober among the crowd which has partaken freely of the sweet Castle wine. She preserves this attitude of extreme composure even after she has read Sortini's letter; her gestures reveal no hint of surprise, disgust, or horror; indeed, it is Olga who notices her tiredness—"how I always loved her when she was tired like this"—the deep exhaustion of one who has in a short moment understood and accepted his fate. Tearing the letter to pieces, Amalia appears to perform a ritual. Yet Olga is not quite correct when she concludes the report of this scene by saying: "This was the morning which decided our fate. I say 'decided,' but every minute of the previous afternoon was just as decisive" (249). The decisive moment was the one when Amalia read in Sortini's eyes a secret, the secret of the Castle.

Whatever this secret may be, it forces her to reject Sortini's summons. To defend her on the ground that she is simply trying to maintain her self-respect[9] is to reduce her to the proportions of a sentimental heroine in a tragedy of middle-class manners. After all, there is no greatness in falling in love with a man of higher social rank, and, being disappointed in the most offensive way, she could be expected to react emotionally to the insult. But Amalia's attitude is informed with heroism. "She stood," says Olga, "face to face with the truth and went on living and endured her life then and now." Her experiences afterward only translate the view that opened itself before her into tangible fact: "We saw only the effects, but she looked down into the bottom" ("Sie sah in den Grund"; *Grund* connoting "ground," "reason," and "cause"—272).

Since it is the Castle's secret she saw there at the bottom of Sortini's eyes, it must remain hidden from K. as well as from the reader. When K. tries to obtain information about Barnabas and the Castle from her, Amalia recoils with unusual violence: "I am not initiated, nothing could induce me to become initiated, nothing at all, not even my consideration for you" (223). This is the voice of a burnt child who has been asked to discuss the nature of fire, and it sounds so convincing that K. ceases plying her with questions. Even he understands that she keeps "her motives locked in her bosom and no one will ever tear

[9] Gray, p. 114.

them away from her" (257–58). Yet she is not prevented from talking by shame or fright—her sharp-sighted eyes have penetrated to regions deeper than her words could ever reach. Its very ineffability identifies Amalia's secret with the mystery of Kafka's Castle.

But whatever horror she saw, it did not destroy her; nor did her defiance of the dreadful prove fatal to her and her house. She goes on living in the village and enduring her life outside the jurisdiction of the Castle. She has scorned authority and has paid her price; K. observes that she has "the ageless look of women who seem not to grow any older, but seem never to have been young either" (267). She stands apart, outside any community, even the most intimate communion of sex; exposed to despair, she faces despair upright and cold, for her eyes have seen beyond it. In the lone figure of this woman Kafka accepted what became to be known after him and partly through him as existential solitude. (Had he been able to divulge the content of Amalia's vision, he could actually be said to have been an existentialist.)

Yet Kafka remained silent. Amalia alone knows what she has seen, and she is only one episode along the path of the Land-Surveyor. She is not even a decisive one by his standards, since he can hardly make use of her. Yet precisely because she refuses to function as his mirror, she is set opposite him to serve him as an example. She demonstrates the possibility of living in this village, neither by right nor by sufferance, but independent of the Castle. Sick and exhausted, she goes on scorning her fate amidst her family, which, while still trying to curry favor with the authorities, is lost in its own labyrinths. She has dragged them down along with herself, and they have become strangers to her. Still, Olga has to admit that "hers is the decisive voice in the family for better or worse" (225). Each emergency is met by her whose very name means "labor";[10] she needs "hardly any sleep, is never alarmed, never afraid, never impatient, she did everything for the parents; while we were fluttering around uneasily without being able to help, she remained cool and quiet whatever happened" (282). Having resigned from all her claims to humanity, she has become a holy sister of despair.

In the image of her sister, Olga inadvertently has shown K. a way to survive the Castle, if not to conquer it. This way would also have led

[10] Rudolf Kleinpaul, *Die deutschen Personennamen* (Leipzig: Göschen, 1909), p. 40. (In a later edition [1924] Kleinpaul modified his opinion, claiming that the name Amalia probably was derived from the French name Amélie, which was first cited in German during the sixteenth century.)

him out of the labyrinth. But he remains blind to the door which opens before him. Having been told Amalia's story, he assures Olga that he prefers her and her ways. "If he had to choose between Olga and Amalia it would not cost him much reflection" (300). With these words he takes his leave of Barnabas' hut and gropes his way back into the darkness. It is, presumably, the darkness of his last night.

The World of Franz Kafka

by Eric Heller

Sometimes I feel I understand the Fall of Man better than anyone.

—Franz Kafka

I

The relationship of Kafka's heroes to that truth for which they so desperately search can best be seen in the image through which Plato, in a famous passage of his *Republic,* expresses man's pitiable ignorance about the true nature of the *Ideas.* Chained to the ground of his cave, with his back toward the light, all he perceives of the fundamental reality of the world is a play of shadows thrown on to the wall of his prison. But for Kafka there is a further complication: perfectly aware of his wretched imprisonment and obsessed with a monomaniac desire to know, the prisoner has, by his unruly behavior and his incessant entreaties, provoked the government of his prison to an act of malicious generosity. In order to satisfy his passion for knowledge they have covered the walls with mirrors which, owing to the curved surface of the cave, distort what they reflect. Now the prisoner sees lucid pictures, definite shapes, clearly recognizable faces, an inexhaustible wealth of detail. His gaze is fixed no longer on empty shades, but on a full reflection of ideal reality. Face to face with the images of Truth, he is yet doubly agonized by their hopeless distortion. With an unparalleled fury of pedantry he observes the curve of every line, the ever-changing countenance of every figure, drawing

"The World of Franz Kafka" by Erich Heller. From The Disinherited Mind *(London: Bowes & Bowes Publishers, Ltd., 1952), pp. 197–231. Copyright 1952 by Erich Heller. Reprinted by permission of Bowes & Bowes Publishers, Ltd. This essay is also reprinted in* Kafka, *ed. Ronald Gray, Twentieth Century Views (Englewood Cliffs, N. J.: Prentice-Hall, Inc., 1962), pp. 99–122.*

schemes of every possible aberration from reality which his mirror may cause, making now this angle and now that the basis of his endless calculation which, he passionately hopes, will finally yield the geometry of truth.

In a letter (December 16, 1911) Kafka says: "I am separated from all things by a hollow space, and I do not even reach to its boundaries." In another (November 19, 1913): "Everything appears to me constructed. . . . I am chasing after constructions. I enter a room, and I find them in a corner, a white tangle." And as late as 1921: "Everything is illusion: family, office, friends, the street, the woman, all illusion, drawing nearer and further away; but the nearest truth is merely that I push my head against the wall of a cell without doors or windows."[1] And in one of his aphorisms he says: "Our art is dazzled blindness before the truth: the light on the grotesquely distorted face is true, but nothing else."[2]

Kafka's novels take place in infinity. Yet their atmosphere is as oppressive as that of those unaired rooms in which so many of their scenes are enacted. For infinity is incompletely defined as the ideal point where two parallels meet. There is yet another place where they come together: the distorting mirror. Thus they carry into the prison-house of their violently distorted union the agony of infinite separation.

It is a Tantalus situation, and in Kafka's work the ancient curse has come to life once more. Kafka says of himself:

> He is thirsty, and is cut off from a spring by a mere clump of bushes. But he is divided against himself: one part overlooks the whole, sees that he is standing here and that the spring is just beside him, but another part notices nothing, has at most a divination that the first part sees all. But as he notices nothing he cannot drink.[3]

Indeed, it was a curse, and not a word of light which called the universe of Kafka's novels into existence. The very day from which it was

[1] Franz Kafka, *Gesammelte Schriften,* edited by Max Brod (Prague, 1937), VI, p. 108. The present, rather confused, state of Kafka editions is unavoidably reflected in my references. Whenever possible, I refer to English translations of his works. Frequently, however, I had to modify the English text, partly for the sake of greater accuracy and partly for the sake of the particular emphasis required in the context of my discussion. Where my references are to the original, the translations are my own.

[2] *The Great Wall of China,* translated by Willa and Edwin Muir (London, 1946), p. 151.

[3] *Ibid.,* p. 140.

made bore the imprint of a malediction before the creator had touched it. He builds to a splendid design, but the curse runs like a vein through every stone. In one of his most revealing parables Kafka shows himself completely aware of this:

> Everything seemed to fit the design of his edifice magnificently. Foreign workmen brought the marble, quarried for the purpose, each block fashioned for its proper place. The stones lifted themselves up and moved along in obedience to his measuring fingers. No edifice ever grew so smoothly as this temple, or rather this temple grew truly in the way in which temples ought to grow. Only that there were cut into every stone, obviously with wonderfully sharpened instruments, clumsy scribblings from the hands of senseless children, or perhaps inscriptions of barbaric mountain-dwellers; mischievous texts, blasphemous, or totally destructive, fixed there for an eternity which was to survive the temple.[4]

It is the reality of the curse that constitutes the ruthlessly compelling logic of Kafka's writings. They defy all attempts at rational interpretation, for Kafka is the least problematic of modern writers. He never thinks in disputable or refutable generalities. His thinking is a reflex movement of his being and shares the irrefutability of all that is. He thinks at an infinite number of removes from the Cartesian *cogito, ergo sum.* Indeed, it sometimes seems that an unknown "It" does all the thinking that matters, the radius of its thought touching the circumference of his existence here and there, causing him infinite pain, bringing his life into question and promising salvation on one condition only: that he should expand his being to bring it within the orbit of that strange Intelligence. The formula has become: "It thinks, and therefore I am not," with only the agony of despair providing overpowering proof that he is alive. He says of himself that he *is* the problem, and "no scholar to be found far and wide." [5]

There is, outside this agony, no reality about which he could entertain or communicate thoughts, nothing apart from the curse of his own separation from that Intelligence. Yet it is a complete world that is to be found within that pain, the exact pattern of creation once more, but this time made of the stuff of which curses are made. Like sorrow in the tenth of Rilke's *Duino Elegies,* despair is given a home of its own in Kafka's works, faithfully made in the image of customary life, but animated by the blast of the curse. This gives to Kafka's writings

[4] *Gesammelte Schriften,* VI, p. 237.
[5] *The Great Wall of China,* p. 145.

their unique quality. Never before has absolute darkness been represented with so much clarity, and the very madness of desperation with so much composure and sobriety. In his work an intolerable spiritual pride is expressed with the legitimate and convincing gesture of humility, disintegration finds its own level of integrity, and impenetrable complexity an all but *sancta simplicitas*. Kafka established the moral law of a boundlessly deceitful world, and performs in a totally incalculable domain ruled by evil demons, the most precise mathematical measurements.

Small wonder at the pathetic plight of critics in the face of Kafka's novels. It was with incredulous amazement that I noticed extracts from reviews which appear as advertisements of the English translation of Kafka's *The Castle*: "One reads it as if one were reading a fairy tale . . ."—"What a lovely, moving, memorable book!"—"A book of curious and original beauty." All this, attributed by the publishers to critics of some repute, is, of course, perverse. A nightmare is not a lovely fairy-tale, and a torture-chamber of the spirit is not full of original beauty. More serious, however, are the misinterpretations of Kafka by those who have undoubtedly made an honest effort to understand him. In the introduction to his own (and Willa Muir's) translation of *The Castle* Edwin Muir describes the subject-matter of this novel (very much in keeping with Max Brod's interpretation) as "human life wherever it is touched by the powers which all religions have acknowledged, by divine law and divine grace," and suggests that it should, with some reservations, be regarded "as a sort of modern *Pilgrim's Progress*," the reservation being that "the progress of the pilgrim here will remain in question all the time." According to him "*The Castle* is, like the *Pilgrim's Progress*, a religious allegory." [6]

From a great number of similar attempts to elucidate the darkness of Kafka's world I am choosing these sentences as a starting-point for a discussion of the work of this writer, and of *The Castle* in particular, because they express most succinctly what seems to me a disquieting misconception of its nature, the more disquieting because it is harbored by men of letters who are seriously concerned with literature and have—like Max Brod, Kafka's lifelong friend and editor of his writings, and Edwin Muir, his English translator—grasped the religious relevance of their author. Thus their misapprehension would seem to reflect a very profound religious confusion, so profound in-

[6] *The Castle,* translated by Willa and Edwin Muir (London, 1947), p. 6.

deed that one can scarcely hold the individual critic responsible for it. It is the very spiritual uprootedness of the age which has deprived us of all sureness of religious discrimination. To men suffering from spiritual starvation, even a rotten fruit of the spirit may taste like bread from Heaven, and the liquid from a poisoned well like the water of life. If the critic is, moreover, steeped in psychology and comparative religion (as we all unwittingly are) the difference may appear negligible to him between Prometheus clamped to the rock, and the martyrdom of a Christian saint; between an ancient curse, and the grace that makes a new man.

The Castle is as much a religious allegory as a photographic likeness of the devil could be said to be an allegory of Evil. Every allegory has an opening into the rarefied air of abstractions, and is furnished with signposts pointing to an ideal construction beyond. *The Castle,* however, is a terminus of soul and mind, a *non plus ultra* of existence. In an allegory the author plays a kind of guessing game with his reader, if he does not actually provide the dictionary himself; but there is no key to *The Castle.* It is true that its reality does not precisely correspond to what is commonly understood in our positivist age as real, namely, neutral sense-perception of objects and, neatly separated from them, feelings; hence our most authentic and "realistic" intellectual pursuits: natural sciences and psychology; and our besetting sins: the ruthlessness of acquisitive techniques and sentimentality. In Kafka's novels there is no such division between the external sphere and the domain of inwardness, and therefore no such reality.

Kafka's creations are at the opposite pole to the writings of that type of Romantic poet, the true poetical representative of the utilitarian age, who distills from a spiritually more and more sterile external reality those elements which are still of some use to the emotions, or else withdraws from its barren fields into the greenhouse vegetation of inwardness. The author of *The Castle* does not select for evocative purposes, nor does he project his inner experience into a carefully chosen timeless setting. He does not, after the manner of Joyce, give away, in the melodious flow of intermittent articulation, the secret bedroom conversations which self conducts with self. There are no private symbols in his work, such as would be found in symbolist writing, no crystallized fragments of inner sensations charged with mysterious significance; nor is there, after the fashion of the Expressionists, any rehearsing of new gestures of the soul, meant to be more in harmony with the "new rhythm" of modern society. Instead of all this, the reader is faced with the shocking spectacle of a miraculously sensitive soul incapable of being reasonable, or cynical, or resigned, or rebellious, about the prospect of eternal damnation. The world which this soul perceives is unmistakably like the reader's own; a castle that is a castle and "symbolizes" merely what all castles symbolize: power and authority; a telephone exchange that produces more muddles than connections; a bureaucracy drowning in a deluge of forms and files; an obscure hierarchy of officialdom making it impossible ever to find the man authorized to deal with a particular case; officials who work overtime and yet get nowhere; numberless interviews which never are to the point; inns where the peasants meet, and barmaids who serve the officials. In fact, it is an excruciatingly familiar world, but reproduced by a creative intelligence which is endowed with the knowledge that it is a world damned for ever. Shakespeare once made one of his characters say:

> They say miracles are past, and we have our philosophical persons, to make modern and familiar things supernatural and causeless. Hence it is that we make trifles of terrors, ensconcing ourselves in seeming knowledge when we should submit ourselves to an unknown fear.

In Kafka we have the abdication of the philosophical persons.

In his work the terror recaptures the trifles, and the unknown fear invades all seeming knowledge—particularly that of psychology. Any criticism of the current religious interpretation of Kafka (which, at least, meets the religious aspect of his work on its own plane) is, I think, well advised to avoid the impression that it sides surreptitiously with other equally well-established dogmas about this writer. One of them, the psychological, is laid down by critics fascinated by Kafka's indubitably strained relationship with his father. But to interpret Kafka's novels in the perspective of the Oedipus complex is about as helpful to our understanding of his work as the statement that Kafka would have been a different person (and perhaps not a writer at all) if he had had another father; a penetrating thought, of which even psychologically less initiated ages might have been capable if they had deemed it worth thinking. This kind of psychology can contribute as much to the explanation of a work of art as ornithological anatomy to the fathoming of a nightingale's song. But so deeply ingrained is positivism in the critics of this age that even when they are genuinely moved by the symbolic reality which the author has created, they will soon regain the balance of mind required for the translation of the symbol into what it "really" means; and by that they mean precisely that meaningless experience which the artist has succeeded in transcending through his poetic creation. If, for instance, to the author the *meaning* of his senselessly tormenting feud with his father has been revealed through the discovery (which, in creating his work, he has made) that what he is *really* called upon to find is his place within a true spiritual order of divine authority, the interpreter will insist that what the author "really" means by talking about God, is that the quarrels with his father should stop.

In Kafka we have before us the modern mind, seemingly self-sufficient, intelligent, sceptical, ironical, splendidly trained for the great game of pretending that the world it comprehends in sterilized sobriety is the only and ultimate reality there is—yet a mind living in sin with the soul of Abraham. Thus he knows two things at once, and both with equal assurance: that there *is* no God, and that there *must* be God. It is the perspective of the curse: the intellect dreaming its dream of absolute freedom, and the soul knowing of its terrible bondage. The conviction of damnation is all that is left of faith, standing out like a rock in a landscape the softer soil of which has been eroded by the critical intellect. Kafka once said: "I ought to welcome eternity, but to find it makes me sad." [7]

This is merely an exhausted echo of the fanfares of despair with which Nietzsche (in many respects a legitimate spiritual ancestor of Kafka) welcomed his vision of eternity. In one of the posthumously published notes on *Zarathustra,* he says about his idea of the Eternal Recurrence: "We have produced the hardest possible thought—now let us create the creature who will accept it lightheartedly and blissfully!" [8] He conceived the Eternal Recurrence as a kind of spiritualized Darwinian test to select for survival the spiritually fittest. This he formulated with the utmost precision: "I perform the great experiment: who can bear the idea of Eternal Recurrence?" [9] And an ever deeper insight into the anatomy of despair we gain from his posthumous aphorisms and epigrams which were assembled by his editors in the two volumes of *The Will to Power,* many of which refer to the idea of Eternal Recurrence: "Let us consider this idea in its most terrifying form: existence, as it is, without meaning or goal,

[7] *Gesammelte Schriften,* VI, p. 231.
[8] *Menschliches, Allzumenschliches,* XIV, p. 179.
[9] *Ibid.,* XIV, p. 187.

but inescapably recurrent, without a finale into nothingness. . . ." [10] Nietzsche's Superman is the creature strong enough to live forever a cursed existence, even to derive from it the Dionysian raptures of tragic acceptance. Nietzsche feels certain that only the Superman could be equal to the horror of a senseless eternity, and perform the great metamorphosis of turning "this most terrifying knowledge" into the terror of superhuman delight. And Kafka? On most of the few occasions when, in his diary, he speaks of happiness, he registers it as the result of a successful transformation of torture into bliss. This is one of his most horrible entries (November 21, 1911): "This morning, after a long time, I again took pleasure in imagining that a knife is turned in my heart." And in 1921, in the account of a dream: "There was bliss in my welcoming, with so deep a sense of freedom, conviction and joy, the punishment when it came." [11] If Nietzsche's Superman is the aesthetic counterbalance to the weight of the curse, then Kafka is its chosen victim. What some of his critics interpret as signs of religious achievement in his later writings, is merely the all engulfing weariness of a Nietzschean Prometheus, which Kafka expressed in the fourth of his Prometheus legends: "Everyone grew weary of the meaningless affair. The gods grew weary, the eagles grew weary, the wound closed wearily." [12]

Thus Kafka's work, as much as Nietzsche's, must remain a stumbling-block to the analysing interpreter to whom, in the enlightened atmosphere of modern Europe, the word "curse" comes only as a faint memory of Greek tragedy, or as a figurative term for a combination of ill-luck and psychological maladjustment. Yet the gray world of Kafka's novels is luminous with its fire. Perhaps one cannot expect from modern man that, when he sees light, he should be able to distinguish between burning sulphur and the radiance of Heaven. And although Mr. Muir is right in saying that Kafka's novels are about life in the grip of a power "which all religions have acknowledged," this power is certainly not "divine law and divine grace," but rather one which, having rebelled against the first and fallen from the second, has, in its own domain, successfully contrived the suspension of both. Undoubtedly, the land surveyor K., hero of *The Castle,* is religiously fascinated by its inscrutably horrid bureaucracy; but again it is a word from Nietzsche, and not from the Gospels, that sums up

[10] *Ibid.,* XVIII, p. 45.
[11] *Gesammelte Schriften,* VI, p. 108.
[12] *The Great Wall of China,* p. 129.

the situation: "Wretched man, your god lies in the dust, broken to fragments, and serpents dwell around him. And now you love even the serpents for his sake."

II

The Castle is not an allegorical, but a symbolic novel. A discussion of the difference could easily deteriorate into pedantry, the more so as, in common and literary usage, the terms are applied rather arbitrarily and have established themselves as meaning more or less the same thing. It will, however, help our understanding of Kafka's work if we distinguish, in using these two terms, two different modes of experience and expression. I shall therefore define my own—probably not less arbitrary—use of the terms.

The symbol *is* what it represents; the allegory represents what, in itself, it is *not*. The terms of reference of an allegory are abstractions; a symbol refers to something specific and concrete. The statue of a blindfolded woman, holding a pair of scales, is an *allegory* of Justice; bread and wine are, for the Christian communicant, *symbols* of the Body and Blood of Christ.[13] Thus an allegory must always be rationally translatable; whether a symbol is translatable or not depends on the fundamental agreement of society on the question of what kind of experience (out of the endless range of possible human experience) it regards as significant. The possibility of allegorizing will only vanish with the last man capable of *thinking in abstractions,* and of forming *images* of them; yet the validity of symbols depends not on rational operations, but on complex experiences in which thought and feeling merge in the act of spiritual comprehension. The sacramental symbols, for instance, would become incommunicable among a race of men who no longer regard the life, death, and resurrection of Christ as spiritually relevant *facts.* An allegory, being the imaginary representation of something abstract, is, as it were, doubly unreal; whereas the symbol, in being what it represents, possesses a double reality.

Goethe, summing up in one line at the end of *Faust II* the mature

[13] At this point I would like to beg the indulgence of the reader for disregarding the established theological terminology. The following discussion will, I hope, to some extent justify my apparent arbitrariness, which I do not wish to maintain outside the scope of this particular argument.

experience of his life, attributes whatever permanent reality there may be in a transient world to its symbolic significance. What is, is only *real* in so far as it is symbolic. Earlier in his life he defined the "true symbol" as "the representation of the general through the particular, not, however, as a dream or shadow, but as the revelation of the unfathomable in a moment filled with life."

The predicament of the symbol in our age is caused by a split between "reality" and what it signifies. There is no more any commonly accepted symbolic or transcendent order of things. What the modern mind perceives as order is established through the tidy relationship between things themselves. In one word: the only conceivable order is positivist-scientific. If there still is a—no doubt, diminishing—demand for the fuller reality of the symbol, then it must be provided for by the unsolicited gifts of art. But in the sphere of art the symbolic substance, dismissed from its disciplined commitments to "reality," dissolves into incoherence, ready to attach itself to any fragment of experience, invading it with irresistible power, so that a pair of boots, or a chair in the painter's attic, or a single tree on a slope which the poet passes, or an obscure inscription in a Venetian church, may suddenly become the precariously unstable center of an otherwise unfocused universe. Since "the great words from the time when what *really* happened was still visible, are no longer for us" (as Rilke once put it in a Requiem for a young poet), the "little words" have to carry an excessive freight of symbolic significance. No wonder that they are slow in delivering it. They are all but incommunicable private symbols, established beyond any doubt as symbols by the quality and intensity of artistic experience behind them, but lacking in any representative properties. Such is the economy of human consciousness that the positivist impoverishment of the one region produces anarchy in the other. In the end, atomic lawlessness is bound to prevail in both.

The intellectual foundation of every human society is a generally accepted model of reality. One of the major intellectual difficulties of human existence is, I think, due to the fact that this model of reality is in every single case a mere *interpretation* of the world, and yet exerts, as long as it seems the valid interpretation, the subtly compelling claim to being accepted as the only true picture of the universe, indeed as truth itself. This difficulty, manifesting itself in the deeper strata of doubt, by which, at all times, certain intellectually sensitive men have been affected, develops easily into a mental epidemic in epochs in which a certain model of reality crumbles and collapses. It seems that we have lived in such an epoch for a long time.

One of its main characteristics was the uncertainty, steadily increasing in the minds and feelings of men, about the relation between mundane and transcendental reality; or, in other words, about the meaning of life and death, the destiny of the soul, the nature and sanction of moral laws, the relative domains of knowledge and faith. As far as Christianity was the representative religion of the Middle Ages, their model of reality was essentially sacramental. A definite correspondence prevailed between the mundane and transcendental spheres. Faith was not established in any distinct "religious experience," nor, as a particular "mode of comprehension," kept apart from "knowledge." It was an element in *all* experience, indeed its crystallizing principle. Only within a mold and pattern determined by faith did experiences make sense and impressions turn to knowledge. This correspondence between the two spheres was so close that at every important stage of man's life they met and became one in the Sacraments.

The sacramental model of reality, intermittently disputed and questioned throughout the whole development of Christian theological thought, was upset in an historically decisive fashion at the time of the Reformation. During that period an intellectual tension, inherent in Christian dogma, developed into a conflagration of vast historical consequences. It produced an articulate climax—which was, however, a mere symptom of a more inarticulate, yet more comprehensive process—at a particularly exposed point of dogmatic faction: the sacramental dispute between Luther and Zwingli. Luther, despite his divergent interpretation of the traditional dogma, represents in it the essentially medieval view, whereas Zwingli, disciple of the humanist Pico della Mirandola, is the spokesman of modernity. To Luther the Sacrament of the Last Supper *is* Christ (the bread and the wine *are* what they represent), while Zwingli reduces it to the status of an allegory (as merely representing what, in itself, it is not). From then onwards the word "merely" has been attaching itself ever more firmly to the word "symbol," soon gaining sufficient strength to bring about a complete alienation between the two spheres. Finally a new order of things emerged. Within it the transcendental realm is allotted the highest honors of the spirit, but, at the same time, skilfully deprived of a considerable measure of reality; the mundane, on the other hand, is recompensed for its lowering in spiritual stature by the chance of absorbing all available reality and becoming more "really" real than before.

The sudden efflorescence of physical science in the seventeenth century is the positive result of this severance. Its successes have further contributed to the "lower realm" setting itself up as the only "really" real one, and as the sole provider of relevant truth, order, and lawfulness. Scientific and other positivist pursuits owe the unchallenged dominion, which they have wielded ever since over the intellectual life of Europe, to the ever more exclusive fascination which the new model of reality has had for the European mind.

As an unavoidable corollary of this state of affairs, religion and art lost their unquestioned birthright in the homeland of human reality, and turned into strange messengers from the higher unreality, admitted now and then as edifying or entertaining songsters at the positivist banquet. What had once been a matter-of-fact expression of life, became a "problem," worthy of a great deal of intellectual fuss and a negligible assignment of reality. As far as the arts are concerned, it is most revealing that the only *distinctive* artistic achievement of Europe since the end of the seventeenth century was accomplished by the art with the least claim to "reality," music; while the most "real" of all arts, architecture, degenerated more and more until it gained new vitality as the unashamed fuctional servant of technology.

In Germany, a country which, for historical reasons too complex ever to be unravelled, suddenly rose in the eighteenth century to the heights of European consciousness and to the fulfillment of the most extravagant intellectual aspirations (without any gradual transition from the Middle Ages), the plight of the poet within the new model of reality is most conspicuous. The artist as an exile from reality—this is one of the most authentic themes of German literature, from Goethe's *Tasso* and Grillparzer's *Sappho* to Thomas Mann's *Tonio Kröger*. Kleist, Hölderlin, Nietzsche are the greatest among the victims of a hopeless collision between the minority demand for a realization of the spirit and a spiritualization of reality on the one hand, and, on the other, the inexorable resistance of a safely established spirit-proof view of life. Hölderlin is the greatest poet among those involuntary desperadoes of the spirit. His work is one continuous attempt to recapture the lost reality of the symbol and the sacramental experience of life. And for Goethe, to preserve his life, exposed at every point to the revengeful blows of the banished spirit, was, from beginning to end, a terrible struggle, entailing the most precarious maneuvers of compromise, irony and resignation. It was only—ironically enough—in his scientific activities that he gave vent to his unrestrained fury against the analytical-positivist view of the world and its scientific exposition through mathematics and Newtonian physics. How gloriously he blundered into physical science, determined to meet the enemy on his own ground, and how stubbornly convinced he was of being right! He once said to Eckermann (February 19, 1829):

> Whatever I have achieved as a poet is nothing to be particularly proud of. Excellent poets are my contemporaries, still better poets lived before me, and others will come after me. But in my own century I am the only man who knows what is right in the difficult science of colors; and this is something that gives me real satisfaction and a feeling of superiority over many.

His own idea of science was based on the *Urphänomen,* a striking assertion of the symbol as the final and irreducible truth of reality.

Goethe lost the battle for the symbol. In the century that stretches between his death and Kafka's writing, reality has been all but completely sealed off against any transcendental intrusion. But in Kafka's work the symbolic substance, forced back in every attempt to attack from above, invades reality from down below, carrying with it the stuff from hell. Or it need not even invade: Kafka writes at the point where the world, having become too heavy with spiritual emptiness, begins to sink into the unsuspected demon-ridden depths of unbelief. In this cataclysm, the more disastrous because it overtakes a world which has not even believed in its own unbelief, Kafka's heroes struggle in vain for spiritual survival. Thus his creations are symbolic, for they are infused with (and not merely allegorical of) negative transcendence.

Kafka knew the symbolic relevance of his work; he knew, too, of the complete alienation of modern man from the reality of the symbol. One of his profoundest meditations runs as follows:

> Many complain that the words of the wise are always merely symbols and of no use in daily life, which is the only life we have. When the wise man says: "Go over," he does not mean that we should cross to some actual place, which we could do anyhow if it were worth the effort; he means some miraculous beyond, something unknown to us, something that he too cannot define more precisely, and therefore cannot help us here in the least. All these symbols merely express that the incomprehensible is incomprehensible, and we have known that before. But the cares we have to struggle with every day: that is a different matter.

Concerning this a man once said: Why such reluctance? If you only followed the symbols you would become symbols yourselves, and thus rid of all your daily cares.

Another said: I bet this is also a symbol.

The first said: You have won.

The second said: But unfortunately only symbolically.

The first said: No, in reality; symbolically you have lost.[14]

III

There are, however, allegorical elements to be found in *The Castle:* for instance, the names of many of the characters. The hero himself, who is introduced to us with the bare initial K. (undoubtedly an autobiographical hint,[15] and at the same time, through its very incompleteness, suggesting an unrealized, almost anonymous personality) is a land-surveyor. Kafka's choice of this profession for his hero clearly has a meaning. The German for it is *Landvermesser,* and its verbal associations are significant. The first is, of course, the land-surveyor's professional activity, consisting precisely in what K. desperately desires and never achieves: to produce a workable order within clearly defined boundaries and limits of earthly life, and to find an acceptable compromise between conflicting claims of possession. But *Vermesser* also alludes to *Vermessenheit, "hubris";* to the adjective *vermessen,* "audacious"; to the verb *sich vermessen,* "commit an act of spiritual pride," *and* also, "apply the wrong measure," "make a mistake in measurement." The most powerful official of the Castle (for K., the highest representative of authority) is called *Klamm,* a sound producing a sense of anxiety amounting almost to claustrophobia, suggesting straits, pincers, chains, clamps, but also a person's oppressive silence. The messenger of the Castle (as it turns out later, self-appointed and officially never recognized) has the name of *Barnabas,* the same as that man of Cyprus who, though not one of the Twelve, came to rank as an apostle; "Son of Consolation," or "Son of Exhortation," is the Biblical meaning of his name, and it is said of him that his exhortation was of the inspiring kind, and so built up faith. And the Barnabas of the novel is indeed a son of consolation, if only in the desperately ironical sense that his family, whom the curse of the

[14] *The Great Wall of China,* p. 132.

[15] The first draft of the novel was written in the first person.

Castle has cast into the lowest depths of misery and wretchedness, in vain expects deliverance through his voluntary service for the authority. To K., however, his messages, in all their obscurity and pointlessness, seem the only real link with the Castle, an elusive glimmer of hope, a will-o'-the-wisp of faith. Barnabas' counterpart is *Momus,* the village secretary of Klamm, and namesake of that depressing creature, the son of Night, whom the Greek gods had authorized to find fault with all things. In the novel it is he whose very existence seems the denial of any hope which Barnabas may have roused in K. *Frieda* ("peace") is the girl through whose love K. seeks to reach the goal of his striving; *Bürgel* (diminutive of *Bürge,* "guarantor"), the name of the little official who offers the solution, without K. even noticing the chance; and the secretary through whom K. does expect to achieve something and achieves nothing, is called *Erlanger* ("citizen of the town of Erlangen," but also suggestive of *erlangen,* "attain," "achieve").

This discussion of names provides an almost complete synopsis of the slender plot of *The Castle.* Someone, a man whose name begins with K., and of whom we know no more, neither whence he comes nor what his past life has been, arrives in a village which is ruled by a Castle. He believes that he has been appointed land-surveyor by the authorities. The few indirect contacts that K. succeeds in establishing with the Castle—a letter he receives, a telephone conversation he overhears, yet another letter, and above all the fact that he is joined by two assistants whom the rulers have assigned to him—*seem* to confirm his appointment. Yet he himself is never fully convinced, and never relaxes in his efforts to make quite sure of it. He feels he must penetrate to the very center of authority and wring from it a kind of ultra-final evidence for his claim. Until then he yields, in paralyzed despair, broken by only momentary outbursts of rebellious pride, to the inarticulate, yet absolutely self-assured refusal of the village to acknowledge him as their land-surveyor:

> You've been taken on as land-surveyor, as you say, but, unfortunately, we have no need of a land-surveyor. There wouldn't be the least use for one here. The frontiers of our little estates are marked out and all neatly registered. . . . So what would be the good of a land-surveyor? [16]

says the village representative to him.

K.'s belief appears, from the very outset, to be based both on truth and illusion. It is Kafka's all but unbelievable achievement to force—

[16] *The Castle,* p. 79.

indeed, to frighten—the reader into unquestioning acceptance of this paradox, presented with ruthless realism and irresistible logic. Truth and illusion are mingled in K.'s central belief in such a way that he is deprived of all order of reality. Truth is permanently on the point of taking off its mask and revealing itself as illusion, illusion in constant danger of being verified as truth. It is the predicament of a man who, endowed with an insatiable appetite for transcendental certainty, finds himself in a world robbed of all spiritual possessions. Thus he is caught in a vicious circle. He cannot accept the world—the village —without first attaining to absolute certainty, and he cannot be certain without first accepting the world. Yet every contact with the world makes a mockery of his search, and the continuance of his search turns the world into a mere encumbrance. After studying the first letter from the Castle, K. contemplates his dilemma:

> . . . whether he preferred to become a village worker with a distinctive but merely apparent connection with the Castle, or an ostensible village worker whose real occupation was determined through the medium of Barnabas.[17]

From the angle of the village all K.'s contacts with the Castle are figments of his imagination:

> "You haven't once up till now come into real contact with our authorities. All those contacts are merely illusory, but owing to your ignorance of the circumstances you take them to be real." [18]

The Castle, on the other hand, seems to take no notice whatever of the reality of K.'s miserable village existence. In the midst of his suffering the indignity of being employed as a kind of footman to the schoolmaster, he receives the following letter from Klamm:

> "The surveying work which you have carried out thus far has my recognition. . . . Do not slacken in your efforts! Bring your work to a successful conclusion. Any interruption would displease me. . . . I shall not forget you." [19]

From all this it would appear that it is, in fact, the village that disobeys the will of the Castle, while defeating K. with the powerful suggestion that he misunderstands the intentions of authority. And yet the authority seems to give its blessing to the defiance of the village,

[17] *Ibid.*, p. 38.
[18] *Ibid.*, p. 95.
[19] *Ibid.*, p. 150.

and to punish K. for his determination to act in accordance with the letter of its orders. In his fanatical obedience it is really he who rebels against the Castle, whereas the village, in its matter-of-fact refusal, lives the life of the law.

Kafka represents the absolute reversal of German idealism. If it is Hegel's final belief that, in the Absolute, truth and existence are one, for Kafka it is precisely through the Absolute that they are forever divided. Truth and existence are mutually exclusive. From his early days onwards it was the keenest wish of Kafka the artist to convey this in works of art; to write in such a way that life, in all its deceptively convincing reality, would be seen as a dream and a nothing before the Absolute:

> Somewhat as if one were to hammer together a table with painful and methodical technical efficiency, and simultaneously do nothing at all, and not in such a way that people could say: "Hammering a table together is really nothing to him," but rather "Hammering a table together is really hammering a table together to him, but at the same time it is nothing," whereby certainly the hammering would have become still bolder, still surer, still more real and, if you will, still more senseless.[20]

This is how Kafka describes the vision of artistic accomplishment which hovered before his mind's eye when, as a young man, he sat one day on the slopes of the Laurenziberg in Prague. Has he, in his later works, achieved this artistic justification of nonentity? Not quite; what was meant to become the lifting of a curse through art, became the artistically perfect realization of it, and what he dreamed of making into something as light as a dream, fell from his hands with the heaviness of a nightmare. Instead of a vindication of nothingness, he achieved the portrayal of the most cunningly vindictive unreality. He had good reason for decreeing that his writings should be burned.

It is hard to see how *The Castle* can possibly be called a religious allegory with a pilgrim of the type of Bunyan's as its hero. Pilgrimage? On the contrary, the most oppressive quality of Kafka's work is the unshakable stability of its central situation. It takes place in a world that knows of no motion, no change, no metamorphosis. Its caterpillars never turn into butterflies, and when the leaves of a tree tremble it is not due to the wind: it is the stirring of a serpent coiled round its branches. There is, in fact, no pilgrimage to be watched in *The Castle,* and the progress not merely "remains in question all the

[20] *The Great Wall of China,* p. 136.

time," but is not even possible, unless we agree to call progress what Kafka once described in his fable of the mouse:

> "Alas," said the mouse, "the world is growing smaller every day. At the beginning it was so big that I was afraid, I kept running and running, and I was glad when at last I saw walls far away to the right and left, but these long walls have narrowed so quickly that I am in the last chamber already, and there in the corner stands the trap that I must run into." "You only need to change your direction," said the cat, and ate it up.[21]

Of the two points on which Kafka and Bunyan, according to Edwin Muir's introduction, are agreed: "that the goal and the road indubitably exist, and that the necessity to find them is urgent," only the second is correct, and indeed, to find them is so urgent for Kafka that life is impossible unless they are found. But do they exist? "There is a goal, but no way; what we call way is only wavering," [22] is what Kafka says about it. And *is* there really a goal for him? This is Kafka's self-reply:

> He feels imprisoned on this earth, he feels constricted; the melancholy, the impotence, the sickness, the feverish fancies of the captive afflict him; no comfort can comfort him, since it is merely comfort, gentle, head-splitting comfort glozing the brutal fact of imprisonment. But if he is asked what he actually wants he cannot reply, for—that is one of his strongest proofs—he has no conception of freedom.[23]

Kafka's hero is the man who *believes* in absolute freedom, but cannot have any conception of it because he *exists* in a world of slavery. Therefore it is not grace and salvation that he seeks, but either his right or—a bargain with the powers. "I don't want any act of favor from the Castle, but my rights," [24] says K. in his interview with the village representative. But convinced of the futility of this expectation, his real hope is based on Frieda, his fiancée and former mistress of Klamm, whom he is obviously prepared to hand back to him "for a price."

In K.'s relationship to Frieda the European story of romantic love has found its epilogue. It is the solid residue left behind by the evaporated perfume of romance, revealing its darkest secret. In ro-

[21] *Ibid.*, p. 133.
[22] *Ibid.*, p. 145.
[23] *Ibid.*, p. 135.
[24] *The Castle*, p. 98.

mantic love, as it has dominated a vast section of European literature ever since the later Middle Ages, individualism, emerging from the ruins of a communal order of the spirit, has found its most powerful means of transcendence. The spiritually more and more autonomous, and therefore more and more lonely individual worships Eros (and his twin deity within the romantic imagination: Death) as the only god capable of breaking down the barriers of his individualist isolation. Therefore love becomes tragedy: overcharged with unmanageable spiritual demands it must needs surge ahead of any human relationship. In its purest manifestations, romantic love is a glorious disaster of the soul, carrying frustration in its wake. For what the romantic lover seeks is not really the beloved. Intermixed with his erotic craving, inarticulate, diffuse, and yet dominating it, is the desire for spiritual salvation. Even a "happy ending" spells profound disillusionment for the romantic expectation. Perhaps it is Strindberg who wrote the last chapter of its history. It is certainly Kafka who wrote its postscript.

For K. loves Frieda—if he loves her at all—entirely for Klamm's sake. This is not only implied in the whole story of K. and Frieda, but explicitly stated by Kafka in several—afterwards deleted—passages of the book. It is contained in the protocol about K.'s life in the village which Momus has drawn up, and in which K. is accused of having made up to Frieda merely because he believed that in her he would win a mistress of Klamm "and so possess a hostage which could only be redeemed at the highest price." [25] On the margin of the protocol there was also "a childishly scrawled drawing of a man holding a girl in his arms; the girl's face was hidden in the man's breast, but he, being much taller, was looking over her shoulders at a paper in his hand on which he was gleefully entering some figures." [26] But perhaps still more conclusive than Momus' clearly hostile interpretation is another deleted passage giving K.'s own reflections on his love for Frieda:

> . . . And soon afterwards—and there was not even time to think—Frieda had entered his life, and with her the belief (a belief which he was quite unable to abandon completely even now) that through her there was established an almost physical connection with Klamm, intimate to the point of whispered communications; perhaps, for the time being, it was only K. who knew of it, but it needed a mere touch, a word,

[25] *Ibid.*, p. 316, in Max Brod's "Additional Note."
[26] *Ibid.*, p. 317.

> a raising of eyes, to reveal itself first to Klamm, but then to everybody, as something unbelievable but yet self-evident by virtue of the irrefutability of life itself, the irrefutability of the embrace of love. . . . What was he without Frieda? A nonentity, staggering after glittering will-o'-the-wisps. . . .[27]

The desperate desire for spiritual certainty is all that is left of romantic love. K. *wills* his love for Frieda because he *wills* his salvation. He is a kind of Pelagius believing that he "can if he ought," yet living in a relentlessly predestined world. This situation produces a theology very much after the model of Gnostic and Manichean beliefs. The incarnation is implicitly denied in an unmitigated loathing of "determined" matter, and the powers which rule are perpetually suspected of an alliance with the devil because they have consented to the creation of such a loathsome world. Heaven is at least at seven removes from the earth, and only begins where no more neighborly relations are possible. There are no real points of contact between divinity and the earth, which is not even touched by divine emanation. Reality is the sovereign domain of strangely unangelic angels, made up of evil and hostility. The tedious task of the soul is, with much wisdom of initiation and often with cunning diplomacy, gradually to bypass the armies of angels and the strong-points of evil, and finally to slip into the remote kingdom of light.

The Castle of Kafka's novel is, as it were, the heavily fortified garrison of a company of Gnostic demons, successfully holding an advanced position against the maneuvers of an impatient soul. I do not know of any conceivable idea of divinity which could justify those interpreters who see in the Castle the residence of "divine law and divine grace." Its officers are totally indifferent to good if they are not positively wicked. Neither in their decrees nor in their activities is there discernible any trace of love, mercy, charity, or majesty. In their icy detachment they inspire certainly no awe, but fear and revulsion. Their servants are a plague to the village, "a wild, unmanageable lot, ruled by their insatiable instincts . . . their shamelessness knows no limits," [28] an anticipation rather of the blackguards who were to become the footmen of European dictators than the office-boys of a divine ministry. Compared to the petty and apparently calculated torture of this tyranny, the gods of Shakespeare's indignation who "kill us for their sport" are at least majestic in their wantonness.

[27] *Gesammelte Schriften,* IV, pp. 380, 381.
[28] *The Castle,* p. 269.

From the very beginning there is an air of indecency, indeed of obscenity, about the inscrutable rule of the Castle. A newcomer in the village, K. meets the teacher in the company of children. He asks her whether she knows the Count and is surprised at the negative answer:

> "What, you don't know the Count?" "Why should I?" replied the teacher in a low tone, and added aloud in French: "Please remember that there are innocent children present." [29]

And, indeed, what an abhorrent rule it is! The souls of women seem to be allowed to enter the next realm if they surrender, as a sort of pass, their bodies to the officials. They are then married off to some nincompoop in the village, with their drab existence rewarded only by occasional flashes of voluptuously blissful memories of their sacrificial sins. Damnation is their lot if they refuse, as happened in the case of Amalia, Barnabas' sister, who brought degradation upon herself and her family by declining the invitation of the official Sortini.

The unfathomable depths of nonsense into which an interpretation can be lured by its own mistaken assumptions is revealed in Max Brod's critical dealings with that crucial point in the story of Barnabas' family. In his epilogue to *The Castle* Max Brod writes:

> The connection between the Castle—that is divine guidance—and the women . . . may appear mysterious and even inexplicable in the Sortini episode, where the official (Heaven) requires the girl to do something obviously immoral and sordid; here a reference to Kierkegaard's *Fear and Trembling* may be of value. . . . The Sortini episode is literally a parallel to Kierkegaard's book, which starts from the fact that God required of Abraham what was really a crime, the sacrifice of his child; and which uses this paradox to establish triumphantly the conclusion that the categories of morality and religion are by no means identical.[30]

This is, for the believer, downright blasphemy, and a critical insult to the intelligence of a reader able to read for himself the Bible, Kierkegaard, and Kafka. The comparison between Kierkegaard and Kafka would indeed be relevant. It might bring home, even to a modern reader, the difference between Purgatory and Hell. For this is the precise relationship between Kierkegaard's *Fear and Trembling* and Kafka's *The Castle*. The sacrifice of Isaac a parallel to Sortini's designs on Amalia? But this means, without any polemical exaggeration, to

[29] *Ibid.*, p. 21.
[30] *Ibid.*, p. 317.

ascribe to the God of Abraham a personal interest in the boy Isaac, worthy rather of a Greek demi-god. Moreover, He having tested Abraham's absolute obedience, did not accept the sacrifice. Yet Sortini (who conveys to Max Brod the idea of divine guidance and Heaven itself) can, to judge by the example of his colleagues, be relied upon not to have summoned Amalia to his bedroom merely to tell her that one does not do such a thing.

To return from the comic escapades of literary criticism to Franz Kafka's novel: the Castle represents neither divine guidance nor Heaven. It is for K. something that is to be conquered, something that bars his way into a purer realm. K.'s antagonism to the Castle becomes clear from the very first pages of the book. This is how he responds to the first telephone conversation about his appointment which, in his presence, is conducted between the Village and the authorities:

> K. pricked up his ears. So the Castle had recognized him as the land-surveyor. That was unpropitious for him, on the one hand, for it meant that the Castle was well-informed about him, had estimated all the probable chances and was taking up the challenge with a smile. On the other hand, however, it was quite propitious, for if his interpretation were right they had underestimated his strength, and he would have more freedom of action than he had dared to hope.[31]

The correspondence between the spiritual structure of *The Castle* and the view of the world systematized into Gnostic and Manichean dogma is indeed striking. There is, however, no reason to assume that Kafka had any special knowledge of those ancient heresies. In their radical dualism they are merely the model systems of a deep-rooted spiritual disposition, asserting itself over and over again in individuals and whole movements. That which is Gnostic and Manichean is, above all, "the face that is filled with loathing and hate" at the sight of physical reality. Kafka refrains from any dealings with nature. There is, apart from the mention of a starry sky, wind and snow, not one description of nature in *The Castle.* Within the human sphere everything that is of the flesh is treated with a sense of nausea and disgust. All the habitations of men are lightless, airless, and dirty. The nuptial embrace between K. and Frieda takes place amidst puddles of beer on the floor of a public bar, the room still filled with the stale smells of an evening's business, while mass prostitution is carried on in the stable of the inn.

[31] *Ibid.*, p. 15.

But Kafka has also found subtler means of conveying his revolt against the "real." One evening K. is waiting in the dark courtyard of the inn for Klamm to emerge from his village room and enter his sleigh. The coachman, noting K., encourages him to wait inside the sleigh and have a drink from one of the bottles kept in the side pockets. K. opens the bottle and smells:

> Involuntarily he smiled, the perfume was so sweet, so caressing, like praise and good words from someone whom one loves very dearly, yet one does not quite know what they are about and has no desire to know, and is simply happy in the knowledge that it is he who is saying them. "Can this be brandy?" K. asked himself doubtfully, and tasted out of curiosity. Yes, surprisingly enough, it was brandy, and it burned and warmed. How strangely it transformed itself, as he drank, from something which was hardly more than a medium of sweet perfume, into a vulgar drink, fit for a coachman! [32]

Whether intentional or not, this profanation of the perfume of a spirit in the process of being "realized," is a wonderfully subtle symbol of a Manichean perspective of the world. And the most telling formula of this Manichean disposition Kafka once found after finishing one of his stories:

> I can still derive some temporary satisfaction from a work of this kind . . . but happiness only if I ever succeed in lifting the world into a sphere pure, true, unchangeable. (Diary note of September 25, 1917)[33]

Is his Castle of that sphere? It is, no doubt, the highest realm K. is capable of perceiving. This is what misled the critics, but not Kafka himself, into equating it with God. But it is certainly not quite irrelevant that in his personal confessions Kafka never, not once, utters the belief that the incessant striving of his spirit was directed towards God, or prompted by *amor Dei*. All the time his soul is preoccupied with the power of Evil; a power so great that God had to retreat before it into purest transcendence, forever out of reach of life. Life itself is the incarnation of Evil: "Knowledge of the diabolical there can be, but not belief in it, for there is nothing more diabolical than what exists." [34]

[32] *Ibid.*, pp. 132, 133.

[33] Quoted by Max Brod as motto to *Franz Kafka, A Biography,* translated by G. Humphreys Roberts (London, 1947).

[34] *The Great Wall of China,* p. 157. [Ronald Gray's Note: This aphorism is rendered in the Definitive Edition, "There can be knowledge of the diabolical, but no belief in it, for more of the diabolical than there is does not exist." *Wedding Preparations,* p. 51. (" . . . *denn mehr Teuflisches, als da ist, gibt es nicht*").]

And then again the reality of life, still identified with Evil, is denied completely: "There is only a spiritual world; what we call the physical world is the evil in the spiritual one. . . ." [35] Thus the idea of final authority, merely by assuming the shape of physical reality in *The Castle,* falls, without the author either willing it or being able to help it, under the spell of Evil. It is the paradox of spiritual absolutism that the slightest touch of concreteness will poison the purest substance of the spirit, and one ray of darkness blot out a world of light.

Yet Kafka is neither a dogmatic follower of the Gnosis nor a Manichee; he is an artist, and although the cursed rule of the Castle is the farthest point of the world to which his wakeful mind can reach, there dawns, at its extreme boundaries, a light, half-suspectingly perceived, half-stubbornly ignored, that comes from things outside the scope of Klamm's authority. K. knows only one thing: that he must come to grips with Klamm; yet at the same time he knows that his very obsession with this thought precludes him from reaching what he mistakenly believes only Klamm can give. He senses dimly that humility and humor would bring him the possession of which he deprives himself by his very striving for it. In Pepi who, for a short time, was promoted to the rank of barmaid in the local inn (and thus to the opportunity of serving beer to Klamm), now trembling at the prospect of losing her position again, K. meets the caricatured embodiment of his own ambition. In giving advice to her he shows a remarkable knowledge of his own disease:

> It is a job like any other, but for you it is the kingdom of Heaven. Therefore you set about your business with exaggerated zeal . . . you tremble for your position, feel constantly persecuted, try by overdoing your friendliness, to win over those who you believe could help you; but you merely annoy and repel them; for what they look for in a bar is peace, and not, on top of their own cares, the anxiety of a barmaid.[36]

And later:

> If I compare myself to you, I suspect that both of us have tried, in too noisy, too childish, too inexperienced a fashion, to get something which is to be had easily and simply through Frieda's matter-of-factness. We are crying and scratching and tossing about, like little children who tug at the tablecloth, but gain nothing, only cause all the nice things to tumble down, making them unobtainable for ever.[37]

[35] *Ibid.*, p. 149.
[36] *Gesammelte Schriften,* IV, p. 353.
[37] *Ibid.*, p. 355.

But it is in K.'s adventure with the Castle official Bürgel that this insight finds its most striking parable. K., summoned in the middle of the night to an interview with the official Erlanger, has, in his weariness and exhaustion, forgotten the number of the right door, and enters (more in the hope of finding an empty bed there than an official of the Castle) another room. There he encounters, lying in bed, the official Bürgel. The ensuing dialogue, or monologue rather, is one of Kafka's greatest feats in the art of melting the solid flesh of a grotesque reality and revealing behind it the anatomic structure of the miraculous. Bürgel promises K. to settle once and for all his affairs in the Castle. K. is not in the least impressed by this offer. He waves it aside as the boast of a dilettante:

> Without knowing anything of the circumstances in which K.'s appointment had been made, and nothing of the difficulties which it met in the Village and in the Castle, and of the complications which had either already arisen or were in the air; without knowing anything of all this, indeed without even showing—and might one not take that for granted with a secretary?—that he had at least a faint notion of it, he offered, by sleight-of-hand, and with the help of a little pad of notepaper, to settle the matter up there.[38]

It is the unbelief of a labyrinthine mind in the very existence of simplicity. And while K. grows ever more weary, Bürgel delivers, in a rapturous crescendo, the message of the miracle: if a man takes a secretary of the Castle by surprise; if, in the middle of the night, the applicant, almost unconscious of what he does, slips, like a tiny grain through a perfect sieve, through the network of difficulties that is spread over all approaches to the center of authority, then the Castle, in the person of this one secretary, must yield to the intruder, indeed must almost force the granting of the request upon the unsuspecting subject: "You believe it cannot happen? You are right, it cannot happen at all. But one night—who can vouch for everything?—it does happen after all." It is an event so rare that it seems to occur merely by virtue of rumor, and even if it does occur, one can, "as it were, render it innocuous by proving to it—and this proof is easy enough—that there is no room for it in this world." [39] And Bürgel goes on with his rhapsody, describing the shattering delight with which a secretary responds to this situation. But when he ends, K. is sound asleep, and,

[38] *Ibid.*, p. 300.
[39] *Ibid.*, pp. 308, 309.

with the conditions of the miracle fulfilled before his eyes, as oblivious of its possibility as he had been in his tortured wakeful pursuit of it.

Indeed, no comfort can be found *within* this world. Yet the power, not only to experience, but poetically to create this world, must have its source *outside*. Only a mind keeping alive in at least one of its recesses the memory of a place where the soul is truly at home, is able to contemplate with such creative vigor the struggles of a soul lost in a hostile land; and only an immensity of goodness can be so helplessly overcome by the vision of the worst of all possible worlds. This is the reason why we are not merely terrified by the despair of this book, but also moved by its sadness, the melancholy of spiritual failure carrying with it a subtle promise.

In one of his most Manichean sayings Kafka speaks of the power of a single crow to destroy the heavens; but, he adds, this "proves nothing against the heavens, for the heavens signify simply: the impossibility of crows." [40] And although these birds swarm ceaselessly around *The Castle,* its builder built it from the impulse to render them impossible. Is it, one wonders, yet another phantom hope in a deluded world that prompts, in the book, a child, a simple girl and a wretched family to turn with a mysteriously messianic expectation to the land-surveyor K.? And makes, on a deleted page of the unfinished manuscript, a mother invite the homeless stranger to her house with the words: "This man should not be allowed to perish"? [41] Or is it perhaps the reflection of a faith, maintained even in the grip of damnation, which Nietzsche once expressed: "Whosoever has built a new heaven has found the strength for it only in his own hell." [42]

[40] *The Great Wall of China,* p. 146.

[41] *Gesammelte Schriften,* IV, p. 428.

[42] Long after this essay was written, I found the following passage in an as yet unpublished letter of Kafka's: "No people sing with such pure voices as those who live in deepest hell; what we take for the song of angels is their song."

Kafka and the Primacy of the Ethical

by Frederick A. Olafson

Current critical estimates of Kafka's achievement fall into two general types. One view is that Kafka is an expositor of the religious life in its starkest, quasi-Kierkegaardian form. The perpetual rebuffs and unresolvable incongruities, in which the search for God eventuates, never react, it is said, upon the theistic assumptions that define the universe within which Kafka's characters move. Even when its two terms are most hopelessly disjoined, the man-God relation remains the keystone of the moral life. On the other view, Kafka's compulsive recurrence to the God-man antithesis begins to make sense only when these theological puzzles are understood as a coded expression of conflicts and neuroses that can be traced in Kafka's personal life. Neither critic denies the presence of religious themes in Kafka's work, although one takes them at face value and the other undercuts them by a psychoanalytic explanation. Both represent Kafka as permanently impaled upon the dilemmas that beset a religious interpretation of the world. One critic regards these dilemmas as in principle inescapable; the other believes that their reality and urgency are borrowed from the psychic conflicts they symbolize. Accordingly, Kafka's persistence in his theistic assumptions will seem heroic to the one and compulsive to the other. But that he does persist; that he is incapable of seeing himself as other than the helplessly inferior term in the God-man relation; and that this incapacity and the lack of moral autonomy it implies carry over into his art and into his conception of his characters—these are assumptions that may fairly be said to be common to critics of both camps.

I wish to challenge this picture of a morally submissive and acquies-

"Kafka and the Primacy of the Ethical" by Frederick A. Olafson. From The Hudson Review, *XIII (1960), 60–73. Reprinted by permission of* The Hudson Review.

cent Kafka. I suggest that far from being a helpless victim of the religious predicament, Kafka was in fact an unusually clear-eyed and lucid commentator upon it and that his commentary is of a kind that requires a degree of critical detachment and moral self-ownership with which he is not usually credited. More specifically, I will argue that careful examination of Kafka's greatest work, *The Castle,* invalidates at almost every point the critical estimates that place Kafka in the currently fashionable line of descent from Kierkegaard to the theologians of crisis. If affiliations of this sort are needed, I submit that one would do better to associate Kafka with those philosophers and moralists who share an aversion to theodicies and defend the autonomy of morals against those who insist on metaphysical or religious sanctions. I know that to associate Kafka with some of the thinkers who most clearly belong to this tradition is to propound a kind of paradox. In Kafka, there is none of the facile irony or *Fortschrittsfröhlichkeit* that distort the liberal rationalist's treatment of religion. Perhaps any assimilation of a writer like Kafka to a well-defined philosophical tradition blurs his special quality in one way or another. The fact remains that the prevailing emphasis on Kafka's affinities with Kierkegaard and his descendants obscures centrally important features of his work. An interpretation that stresses the very different affinities suggested above can at least sensitize us to much in Kafka that is missed when his intellectual pedigree is antecedently fixed in the manner described.

II

In the relevant sense, a religious view of the world consists in the belief that there exists an all-encompassing purposive order which an all-powerful being, God, progressively realizes; and that this order, however inscrutable, is normative for human beings. When a discrepancy is established between a judgment derived from a human code of morals and the divine program, it is our judgment that must be modified and the human will that must be brought into harmony with the divine will. Within a well-developed religious tradition, a highly selective set of criteria determines what is to be allowed to count as indicative of God's purposes; and frequently a number of moral principles are built into the criteria themselves. Thus, what cannot satisfy an antecedently adopted moral standard cannot count as an expression of God's will. But these rigged definitions still leave us confronted by a great many features of the world which are not allowed by our restrictive criteria to count as expressions of God's will, but which, nevertheless, as their undeniable presence implies, must be at least tolerated by God. Under these circumstances, the pressure to modify the criteria we used in deducing that it would be better if such things did not happen becomes very great. They have happened; and our general assumption of a moral government of the world lends this occurrence an authority that necessitates a revision of the criteria we used. Since we can have no advance guarantees of what the course of the world will be, no antecedent limits can be set to this process of revision.

If such a "teleological suspension of the ethical," of which the story of Abraham and Isaac provide the paradigm case, resolves the conflict unambiguously in favor of the divine, other responses to Abraham's situation are possible. One can, for example, resolve the conflict in such a way that any non-human purposive order becomes irrelevant except in so far as it squares with some human ideal. This anti-Kierkegaardian and anti-revisionist view received its classical formulation from J. S. Mill:

> If I am informed that the world is ruled by a being whose attributes are infinite, but what they are we cannot learn, nor what the principles of his government, except that "the highest human morality of which we are capable of conceiving" does not sanction them, I will bear my fate as I may. But when I am told that I must believe this, and at the same time call this being by the names which express and affirm the highest human morality, I say in plain terms that I will not. I will call no being good who is not what I mean when I apply that epithet to my fellow-creatures; and if such a being can sentence me to hell for not so calling him, to hell I will go.

This passage unmistakably places Mill in the tradition with which I have suggested that Kafka be associated, but it is incidentally characterized by a robust self-confidence, if not by a somewhat theatrical bravado. By anticipation, one may wonder whether, without these special accompanying features and the peculiar ethos they suggest, a refusal essentially like Mill's is not imaginable.

The forthrightness of both these responses to the religious dilemma limits their appeal. For less absolute nature there is a third alternative, although it is not often plainly stated. It is to make the best of both worlds by accepting, on the one hand, the general proposition that the course of the world makes sense, while at the same time operating with a shifting set of criteria for determining what that sense is, with the net result that the sharpest conflicts between the actual course of events and one's intuitive sense of justice are avoided. Characterized in logical terms, this practice consists in so scrambling one's evidential procedures that any state of affairs is made compatible with the truth of the higher-order principle that a divine purpose is being realized. As I hope to show, this third alternative amounts to a kind of logical pragmatism *à outrance* which subordinates everything to the objective of making the higher-order principle come out true under all circumstances and justifies any reassignment of truth-values, however arbitrary, to the premises of an argument endangering that principle, provided the latter is effectively protected. I suggest that the moral world we encounter in *The Castle* is comprehensible only if this uneasy *ménage à trois*—human norms trying to cohabit logically with the actual course of the world and the general covering assumption referred to above—is kept firmly in mind as a term of comparison.

III

The characters in *The Castle* fall into three main groups: K., the stranger who claims that he has been engaged by the Castle as a land-surveyor; the officials of the Castle administration; and the villagers. In most critical treatments of the novel, primary emphasis is placed rightly upon the relation of K. to the Castle. K's relation to the Castle *is* the central issue. It does not follow, however, that the village and its inhabitants are simply a kind of back-drop against which the fundamental conflict between K. and the Castle is played out. The truth is that K.'s relation to the Castle can be understood only if it is contrasted with another, and very different, relationship to the Castle: that of the villagers. More importantly, one can understand Kafka's attitude toward K. and therefore *his* relation to the Castle only if the relative moral weights he assigns to the one and the other relationships are established. What I am suggesting is that the operative moral contrast in the novel is the one between K. and the villagers; that the contrast is unambiguously in K.'s favor; and that these two facts compel a revision of the standard interpretations of Kafka's moral and religious intentions in this novel.

When critics have paid any attention at all to the role of the villagers in the novel, they have tended to idealize them and their way of life. They have what K. does not have and is trying, unsuccessfully, to get. K. is the homeless, alienated, urban man of the modern age and the village symbolizes the organic, pre-individualistic community of an earlier day. K. does in fact want to acquire an accepted status in the community and in pursuit of this goal he is willing to put up with a long series of humiliations; and to that extent, it is true that the villagers' mode of life functions as a kind of ideal in the novel. But if one tries to explain just why it is that K. cannot be accepted by the villagers, things begin to look very different. It turns out that he is unassimilable because he stubbornly persists in certain ways of viewing his own situation, which simply do not lend themselves to the kind of simplistic contrast with the mores of the village that is implicit in an idealizing interpretation.

It is particularly interesting that these differences of attitude are presented, not just as functions of differing local circumstances, but as springing from opposed modes of thought—*Denkweisen*—and by implication, from profoundly different conceptions of the moral life. Early in the novel, in the course of several conversations between K. and various villagers, they emerge in a very explicit way. Indeed, the villagers themselves are aware that there are differences of *Denkweise* and repeatedly say as much. On one occasion, the landlady says to K., after trying to explain to him the ways of the Castle: "If I try very hard, I can, of course, think myself into your ideas, valid, perhaps, in the very different land from which you come." But K.'s notions are "madness, absolute madness; one begins to feel confused when one plays with such mad ideas." K's "ignorance of the actual situation is so appalling that it makes my head go round to listen to you and compare your ideas and opinions with the real state of things."

Specifically, the situation that is interpreted in such diverse ways by K. and by the villagers is the one produced by K.'s presence in the village and his demand that his appointment as land-surveyor be confirmed by the Castle. In K.'s view, this is a straightforward moral situation. The Castle has entered into a quasi-contractual agreement with him, and now that he has, at considerable inconvenience to himself, arrived in the village, the Castle must carry out its part of the bargain. When it seems that his status may not be recognized, K. unhesitatingly makes an approach to the Castle to insist, as he says, "on his rights."

It is of central importance that K. never wavers in his characterization of his own case as a *prima facie* violation of a moral rule—the rule that obliges us to keep our promises. Working, as he does, within a definite system of moral rules, K. assumes that the authority that has the power to set right the wrong that has been done him operates within the same body of rules and need only have the circumstances of the case brought to its attention to correct its error. If it refuses, it will be unmistakably in the wrong. With the exception of one or two passages which I will take up later, everything in the novel indicates that K. recognizes the Castle as the legitimate authority in the village; and any challenge to it that he may represent is one of which he can hardly be said to be aware. But the authority K. recognizes is one that is subject to moral rules and its acts cannot be justified automatically by virtue of the fact that they are acts of the Castle. K. is never tempted to manipulate his argument so as to save the general principle that what the Castle does is right by rejecting the factual premise that in this case it has done wrong. In the last instance, he is prepared to sacrifice the postulate of the infallibility of the Castle and stand by his own moral evaluation of his case.

K.'s conversation with the Mayor makes it plain that the latter would resolve the conflict in a very different way. The Mayor tells K. that "not only is nothing done here without taking thought," but also that "the very possibility of error must be ruled out of account." Later he admits that "once in a while an error does occur as in your case," but he covers himself by asking, "Who can finally say that it is an error?" The implication is that no one can and that in the village no one does. This amounts to saying that when the application of a moral rule to a particular case produces a conclusion that is inconsistent with the principle that what the Castle does is right, it is this conclusion that must be surrendered. The Mayor's way of putting this makes it clear that he, too, has reached the conclusion that there has been an "error" in K.'s case, but the automatic way in which this conclusion is then suppressed illustrates the hermetic, self-sealing character of the moral world which he and the other villagers inhabit. If this procedure seems cynical, it is not a conscious cynicism. To the Mayor, the logical barriers insulating the assumption that the Castle is always right against unfavorable evidence are not artificially contrived. They are as antecedent to reasoning and immune to correction as the assumption they protect. But while the Mayor retires behind these remarkable defenses, K. perseveres in his publicly announced belief that "a terrible abuse of my case, and probably of the law, is being carried on," and threatens that he "will know how to protect (himself) against it."

It is now clear in what sense K. represents a danger to the villagers. Because he persists in viewing his case as a miscarriage of justice, he revives in the villagers the tensions that are produced by a felt inconsistency between their general assumption that the Castle is always right and the perhaps never quite suppressed deliverance of their own moral consciousness. K.'s attitude amounts to a kind of moral aggression against the villagers and he is, by his very presence and his unconscionably simple-minded demands, challenging the moral structure of village life. What is it the villagers are afraid of? They are afraid of moral freedom. If K. can be called in one sense an alienated man, the villagers are alienated in another and profounder sense. In revising their own moral judgments so that they will square with the actions of the Castle (which can never be reduced to a rule), they have alienated their own moral autonomy. They have projected their own moral center of gravity into a remote and incomprehensible agency which is really just a grandiose, externalized image of their own moral *Unmündigkeit.* And having created the Castle, they must protect it against aggressors like K., because in protecting it they are protecting themselves. As K. shrewdly asks, when he is warned by the landlady of what may happen to him if he persists in trying to see Klamm, a high official of the Castle: "What are you afraid of? Surely you are not afraid for Klamm?"

K.'s moral impact is felt, not merely by the village as a whole, but also by specific individuals, and most deeply by Frieda, who becomes K.'s fiancée. Theological critics have seen in the story of K's relationship with Frieda a critique of the romantic conception of love as a mediating link with the divine. Some critics have even regarded this relationship as constituting K.'s "sin." This view is evidently attractive because it seems to provide a justification for the Castle's treatment of K., but it is implausible on two grounds. It is by no means clear that K.'s intentions in this affair are bad. There is a good deal of evidence in the novel that K. and Frieda genuinely love one another; and even if K.'s original motive is to establish contact with the Castle through Frieda, his interest in her should come to an abrupt end when she loses her job in the inn. In fact, his tenderness and affection for her seem to increase. And even if one were to agree that K.'s motives are bad and that he deserves punishment, the "punishment" meted out would still be outrageously disproportionate to the "sin."

The story of K. and Frieda is susceptible of a quite different interpretation. It can be read as a study of the disintegrating effect, upon a person like Frieda, of contact with a person morally organized in the way K. is; and also, perhaps, as a parable of the inability of the morally unfree to love another human being.

To the villagers, Frieda is an enterprising and aggressive young woman, but Kafka repeatedly emphasizes her extreme and even pathetic moral dependence. Her sense of self and her feeling of superiority are based entirely upon the status that her job at the inn gives her and her contact with Klamm, an official of the Castle. But loving K. means sharing his lonely and exposed position in a hostile community; and Frieda is not strong enough to resist these new pressures. She cannot bear separation from Klamm and the loss of her place in the scheme of things that culminates in the Castle. It is remarkable that K., in the midst of his own difficulties, is able to understand the character of this unhappiness and even sympathize with it. As he says to Frieda: "You were torn away from Klamm; I can't calculate how much that meant, but a vague idea of it I've managed to form gradually." At the same time, he urges her "to put the past and its illusions behind you; and to love and trust me as I love you." Frieda responds to his appeals, but in the end the pull of the village is too strong for her. Her last words to K. are: "Why do you always persecute me?" And she adds, "Only think, Jeremiah, he has disproved everything. But even if everything were disproved, what would be gained by that, what would it matter to me?" There could scarcely be a more radical formula of self-disqualification as an independent moral consciousness.

It is significant that in rejecting K., Frieda should turn to one of the "helpers." Their role in the novel is to represent an extreme form of the unconcerned and irresponsible "naturalness" with which K.'s attitude is in such marked contrast. As K. describes them to Frieda, they are "in appearance, good, childish, irresponsible youths, fallen from the sky, from the Castle, a dash of childhood memories with them, too." K. quite explicitly states that "I was the antithesis of it all." In this connection, it is important to note that K. is severe and even cruel in his treatment of the helpers and that Frieda is, by contrast, markedly sympathetic. It is, in fact, hard to deny them a certain amount of sympathy. They are playful and good-humored and cheerfully put up with a great deal of bad treatment. At the same time, there is something pathetic and animal-like about them; and it is impossible to see anything remotely like an idealization of the "natural" in Kafka's description of their antics. They were sent by the Castle "to cheer (K.) up a little" because he "takes things too seriously." They have failed and their encounter with K. has embittered them. But while one may pity them, one cannot regard them as full-fledged persons and certainly not as representing any kind of moral alternative to K. But if the contrast between K. and the villagers is such as I have suggested, then not only does any interpretation that idealizes the villagers fall to the ground, but so does any reading that overlooks the contrast and imputes to K. the attitudes and the role that are in fact those of the villagers.

K.'s harshness toward the helpers may be explained if one remembers that, if he is a danger to the village, the village, in a different way, is a danger, or rather, a temptation to him. There is a remarkable scene in which K. is waiting for Klamm to appear. Klamm's driver offers him a drink of brandy. K. is tempted to relax his watchfulness and to let himself enjoy the obliviousness produced by the brandy which is "so sweet, so caressing, like words of praise from someone one likes very much, yet does not know clearly what they are for and has no desire to know and is simply happy to know it is one's friends who are saying them." What this passage conveys is a sense of the insidious attraction that the villagers' mode of life has for K., and it is this very attraction that obliges him to react harshly to the innocent prankishness of the helpers. To acquiesce in the general mood of uncritical acceptance would be moral suicide for K.; and when he is told that he will miss Klamm whether he waits or not, he replies that he will wait just the same. "It seemed to K. that . . . he had won a freedom such as hardly anybody had ever succeeded in winning, and as if nobody could dare to touch him or drive him away—or even to speak to him; but this conviction was equally strong—as if at the same time there were nothing more senseless, nothing more hopeless than this freedom, this waiting, this inviolability."

IV

Although relatively little critical attention has been paid to the place of the Barnabas family in the novel, K.'s relationship with this family and the story of the family itself are recounted in great detail by Kafka. The reason for this emphasis is to be found in the peculiarly isolated position of the family in the village. By allying himself with the Barnabas family against the village, K. in effect espouses their cause and, in so doing, further defines the difference between himself and the villagers upon which I have been insisting. As Kafka presents it, this episode is so morally unambiguous that it serves as an ideal touchstone for evaluating the sharply different reactions to its central events which he assigns to K. and to the villagers.

The "fate" of the Barnabas family is decided when the older sister, Amalia, angrily rejects a dishonorable proposal made to her by Sortini, a high official of the Castle. Her action, amounting as it does to an independent moral initiative on her part, brings down a punishment on the whole family, but this punishment is not inflicted by the Castle. It is the villagers who, without any apparent prompting, immediately ostracize the Barnabas family. The profound irony of the situation is that if the members of the family did not feel and act guilty, they would not be avoided by the villagers. In the eyes of the latter, any unresolved moral conflict with the Castle is an intolerable solecism and one gathers that they would be satisfied if the Barnabas family would simply act as though amends had been made to the Castle so that the community would be spared the painful spectacle of what looks dangerously like moral autonomy. But, with the possible exception of Amalia, they *do* feel guilty. Of Amalia, who despises "Castle gossip" and does not "know fear, for herself or others," we are told that she can "stand face to face with the truth and go on living." But she is so totally withdrawn that any general challenge to the Castle that may be implicit in her attitude remains undeveloped.

When K. hears the story of the Barnabas family, his reaction is direct and unequivocal. He does not hesitate to qualify Sortini's conduct as "criminal" and the treatment of the family by the villagers as unjust and monstrous. It is not Amalia but "Sortini who horrifies (K.)—the possibility of such abuse of power." He is deeply shocked when Amalia's sister, Olga, seems to suggest that Amalia would have done better to go to Sortini, and he tells Olga that the villagers' reverence for the Castle is "a mistaken reverence,—a reverence that dishonors its object." When Olga tells him that he is the only one in the village who thinks this way, K. replies: "Since nothing has happened, what is there to be afraid of?" In a deleted passage he tells Olga that "it is as though all your endeavors were aimed at establishing the victory of the Castle beyond any doubt." And in another, he explicitly identifies his situation with that of the Barnabas family when he says: "If they are playing a game with you, then they are playing a game with me quite as much, and it is a single, astonishingly unitary game." It should be noted, however, that if Amalia and, by implication, K. fail this test, there are those in the novel who do not. If there is one thing for which the villagers are ready at virtually any hour of the day or night, it is a teleological suspension of the ethical. It follows that the vital question must be whether Kafka gives any clues as to how he evaluates these two utterly different reactions to Sortini's proposal. I submit that there is not a single passage in which any qualification of K.'s initial reaction to the Sortini incident is proposed or in which his original characterization of Sortini's conduct is undercut by a Kierkegaardian line of reasoning. The primary values of the story, as first told, are allowed to stand and the implicit criticism is directed, not at Amalia or K., but at the moral passivity and fearfulness of the villagers.

In the course of the Barnabas episode and elsewhere, it becomes apparent that, in spite of K.'s precarious situation, he is looked to by a number of villagers as a source of hope. K.'s interest in the Barnabas family is aroused by the hope that they may help him to establish contact with the Castle; but it turns out that it is they who are looking to him for help. Olga, in fact, tells him that her family's "fate has become in a certain measure dependent upon you." K.'s is in a sense a test case; and his unequivocal insistence on his rights attracts, at the same time as it rather frightens, her. Nor is she the only one to feel this attraction. In his search for intermediaries, K.'s interest is aroused by a woman who is described to him as "a girl from the Castle." She is ill; it is the "climate here that she cannot stand." One may guess that it is the moral climate of the village that she finds intolerable. But she, too, is deeply interested in K. who is significantly described as having "some medical knowledge . . . experience in dealing with sick people." Here, as in the case of the Barnabas family, the roles are reversed; and Hans, her son, who is in the habit of asking insistent questions "to enable him to come to an independent decision about what to do," turns out to be a great admirer of K. He believes that "though for the moment K. was wretched and looked down on, yet in some unimaginable and distant future he would excel everyone." He himself "wants to be a man like K."

Surely it is indicative of Kafka's intentions that these people who are at odds with the village and look hopefully to K. are among the few genuinely sympathetic characters in the novel. To conclude that it is K. and the tiny minority who "side" with him that must learn to emulate the moral docility of the villagers would be a perverse misreading of these intentions. It is well known that Kafka read and was deeply impressed by Kierkegaard's *Fear and Trembling.* But if the story of Abraham was in his mind when he wrote *The Castle,* that story had undergone a remarkable transformation. It is as though Abraham had become convinced that God cannot actually wish him to sacrifice Isaac, and had set out to have an administrative error corrected by the heavenly bureaucracy. But such an Abraham would represent the primacy of the ethical and would be the exact reverse of Kierkegaard's Abraham. If a parallel is drawn to *The Castle* at all, it must be drawn in such a way as to subvert the very thesis it is intended to support.

V

There are two episodes in the novel which seem to resist the general interpretation I am proposing. They are K.'s prematurely combative behavior upon arrival in the village, which suggests that he may be an imposter, and the interview with Bürgel, a liaison secretary of the Castle, in which hope is held out that K.'s petition may be granted.

It is noteworthy that after the first chapter or so, K.'s conduct seems entirely consistent with what one would expect of a man who had come to the village in the honest conviction that he had been appointed land-surveyor there. Why, then, does he strike such a challenging note at the beginning? I have already pointed out that K. does not seem to be fully aware of the nature of the challenge that he represents to the moral structure of the village. Certainly, he has not deliberately come to the village to make that challenge. But if K. does not see all the implications of the stand he is taking, Kafka must. I would argue that the early passages in which K.'s aggressive and suspicious manner seems out of proportion with anything the Castle has done, illustrate a way of presenting K. as himself in possession of an author's-eye view of his role and that this is a mode of presentation that Kafka abandoned and might have been expected to suppress entirely in a final draft of the novel. As evidence, I would point to an alternate version of the opening scene which Kafka *did* delete. Here the challenging attitude I have alluded to appears in greatly intensified form. K. is a man with a mission and it is a mission which has nothing discernible to do with land-surveying, "I am here to fight," he says. "I have a difficult task ahead of me and I have dedicated my whole life to it. I ruthlessly suppress everything that might disturb me in carrying it out." These are the sentiments of a man who is motivated by an abstractly conceived cause of some sort and is deliberately attacking the Castle, and not those of a man who has been unjustly treated and is demanding redress. Kafka must have perceived that a presentation of K. in this latter role would be much more effective than in the former, and one can only agree that it is. One might also suggest, in explanation of these apparent inconsistencies, that, even in this role, K.'s naiveté is never quite complete and that he has flashes of insight into the true nature of the incompatibility of his moral style with that of the village. He seeks an identity in life that can be established only if it is certified by a supreme validating agency, the Castle. But perhaps it is borne in upon him, from time to time, that in this sense, no one has an identity and that in this sense he is not and cannot be a land-surveyor or, indeed, anything at all.

The substance of Bürgel's remarks to K. is that if an official of the Castle is surprised by a petitioner, at night, he is sometimes "involuntarily inclined to judge matters from a more private point of view." A "peculiar and absolutely improper exchange of roles" takes place and errors are committed which are difficult if not impossible to correct. It sounds very much as though Bürgel is describing his own circumstances, inviting K. to make his request, and assuring him that it will be granted. But K. is asleep and does not hear.

Now if Bürgel means what he says and is capable of making good his implied promise, then it certainly seems that a kind of hope has been held out to K. But to whose credit should this redound? Surely not to that of the Castle. By its standards, such actions are mistakes and they occur only when officials improperly judge a case from a "private point of view," i.e., by non-official, "human" standards. In any case, Kafka, on several occasions, emphasizes the relative insignificance of Bürgel's position in the Castle hierarchy and one wonders whether the hope he holds out is not to be classed with the letter and the telephone call from the Castle which seem to assure recognition by the Castle and then turn out to mean little or nothing. Even if Bürgel *is* in a position to hold out the prospect of a reconciliation with the Castle, it is significant that there is no suggestion that K. must first admit some sort of guilt or do penance. In fact, Bürgel's offer is so devoid of conditions that one is tempted to attribute it, as he himself does, to a kind of helplessness on his part that has very little to do with the merits of the case. In any event, the potential recipient of this bemused act of grace is asleep and does not know that an offer is being made, so the danger of a real breach in the Castle system is not very great. Bürgel virtually says as much when he remarks that K.'s sleepiness is "an excellent arrangement" whereby "the world corrects itself in its course and maintains a balance," i.e., cancels out "errors" produced by the helpless benevolence of minor officials and preserves the integrity of the Castle's system. But if so, Bürgel seems rather a part of the system itself, not an alternative to it. In the end, had the novel been completed, K. was to die, exhausted by his efforts which had not produced any result except an edict of the Castle to the effect that although K. had no right to live and work in the village, his presence there would be tolerated. But early in the novel K. explicitly declared that he "did not want an act of grace by the Castle but his rights" and this is what no one in the Castle—not even Bürgel—is prepared to give him.

VI

Could a mind that was permanently immured in the paradoxes of religious faith and incapable of envisaging human action except through the categories and assumptions of such a faith, have had the power to create an imaginative contrast such as that between K. and the villagers? And if it is true that no one could have rendered the moral atmosphere of the village who had not known, in his own life, the meaning of what Kant, in another connection, called the heteronomy of the will, is it not equally true that the conception of such a character as K. presupposes the achievement of a sense of moral identity that lifts the self out of the impasse in which all attempts at theodicy end? If the answer in both cases is affirmative, as I think it must be, then *The Castle* is not a testament of neurosis, but of a painfully won freedom or perhaps of a freedom that is not so much won as accepted. If Kafka begins by believing, with the theologians of crisis, that God is inscrutable, he ends by pushing the man-God contrast to the point where the opacity of the divine intention cancels out its moral relevance. The result is that if one says that God is inscrutable, one must really mean just that and not subtly manipulate this *non possumus* in the interest of some special conception of God's program. Indeed, a consistently agnostic theism and a flat atheism have very much the same effect: to cut off religious discourse and to compel us to make do with such knowledge and with such moral insights as may be otherwise available. If Kafka can be said to be a theist at all then his is a self-diremptive theism. The unique value of his writings derives from the fact that we can almost see their author crossing the invisible line that distinguishes an utterance of the type, "God is inscrutable," that still retains genuine religious significance, from a use of the same formula that makes it no more than a dramatic image for the moral obscurity of the world—not so very different from Nietzsche's "God is dead." Unlike Nietzsche, Kafka never produced a rhetoric of self-assertive moral freedom, and he completely avoids the traditional flourishes of programmatic atheism. On the other hand, it is his great distinction that, having passed this point of no return, he never tried, as so many contemporary Protestant theologians have, to make failure edifying or inscrutability informative. Kafka's spiritual posture is so rare and so hard to define just because he does scrupulously avoid both these kinds of pathos—the pathos of Promethean moral heroism and the pathos of faith "quia absurdum." But what he does do, and what he could hardly have done if his main concern had been Nietzsche's or Kierkegaard's, is to realize, with an authenticity and simple truth that seem to me unique, that crucial moment in the religious life in which the moral consciousness "prises itself off the world" and recognizes itself for the first time in all its vulnerability and precariousness.

K. and the Sacrifice of Intellect

by Günther Anders

THE RELIGIOUS MEANING OF KAFKA'S WORLD. THE THEME OF ARRIVAL

Religious vision. This phrase will command ready assent among those many critics who are only too eager to foist some kind of religious interpretation on Kafka's work. Yet here, above all, we must guard against misunderstanding. If Kafka's world is transfigured it is not with the radiance of eternity; for him it is the very temporal, commonplace world which has become "infinitely" remote, inaccessible, mysterious. And this because *he* (or his hero K.) stands so far outside it, that the "here-and-now" assumes the character of a "beyond." Not, however (and the point should be stressed), the character of an ultimate paradise to be attained, least of all in the "worldly" sense of a Utopian Socialist future. In no sense is it the world to come which is Kafka's "beyond," but the *actual* world. In the same way he "who is to come" is himself, the alien; it is he who has yet to arrive in the world, and to make himself part of the world. Kafka's greatest work, *The Castle,* provides the most striking illustration of this theme.

The story of *The Castle* is quickly told. A man called K. has ostensibly been called to take up a job in a village where there is a castle. He arrives one evening in this village wishing to occupy his allocated position. But those who have summoned him know nothing of his appointment: so he is not accepted, yet neither is he definitely turned away. The rest of his life—and the remainder of the book—

"K. and the Sacrifice of Intellect" (editor's title), from Günther Anders, Franz Kafka, *Chapter I, "The Alien World," trans. by A. Steer and A. K. Thorlby (London: Bowes & Bowes Publishers, Ltd., 1960) pp. 21–23, 28–30.*

is spent in his ever-repeated attempts to get himself accepted nevertheless. It is as if his whole life were a continuous struggle to be born, an endless coming into the world.

The tremendous tension that exists in all true religions between the earthly and the celestial spheres, or between creature and creator—the tension we call *transcendence*—exists here between K. and the world, which since it is a totally institutionalized, indeed, a totalitarian, world of authority, remains inaccessible to him. Thus K. does not "live" (if we take Heidegger's definition of living as "being in the world"); he merely passes his days waiting in attendance on the capricious authority of the masterful world within. He is just sufficiently in the world to realize how deeply he is excluded from it. Many of Kafka's fables as well as his novel *America* begin with scenes of arrival rather like the one in *The Castle*; and each of these attempts to arrive ends in failure. "I no longer have the illusion that everything is only a beginning, or has not yet begun . . ." (Diary, 122, 1921). And 1922: "In my office people still calculate as if my life were really only just beginning, but meanwhile I have come to the end of it."

THE NON-EXISTENT HERO

. . . The possibility that the newcomer might be right in suspecting that customs are in fact decrees, that the rationalist might in fact have an insight into *truth,* is an idea which Kafka never expresses. For him the newcomer is always wrong, on principle, for in a way Kafka sees the problem of the alien, the newcomer, the Jew, through the eyes of those who do not accept the alien. Thus, Kafka is a rationalist ashamed of his own position—like all those Jews who try to conform to the customs and habits of a country whose constitution does not proclaim the rationalistic recognition of the rights of every man, the alien included, *as a man.* Those who are indisputably children of the society, of the Castle-village, accept without hesitation what society decrees—its customs—as synonymous with *morality*; for them ἐθος and ἦθος are one. Here Kafka glimpses what Nietzsche called "the first phase" of morality: the morality of customs. It does not matter that he could not *actually* have seen this primitive condition still existing anywhere in the modern world. For Kafka is describing the normal world from the outside; from the standpoint of those to whom its *mores* will necessarily appear at first to have nothing whatever to do with rational morality. To such an outsider it will seem that he has somehow to learn the secret of identifying these two spheres completely (just as we all wish to do on arriving in a foreign country). And Kafka stresses this identification by saying of the inhabitants of the village that for them loving and obeying—the psychological correlatives of "what is" and "what should be"—are one and the same thing. "We know," says Olga, one of the village girls, that women cannot help loving officials if these once turn their attention towards them"—i.e. there is no difference between the objective event and the subjective judgment of it, for any division of the two spheres is quite incomprehensible to the fully integrated individual. Indeed, any differentiation between "being" and "being conscious," between εθος and ἦθος, between what *is* and what *should be,* is always revolutionary. Furthermore, this is the natural reaction of the newcomer who makes demands for which, in the customs of the village, no provision has been made. This is why immigrants so frequently belong to radical movements; they agitate for the recognition of the rights of the unrecognized.

But once a distinction has been made between customs and morals, it cannot be revoked without serious consequences, though thousands, in their effort to belong, have placed themselves in a most paradoxical position by attempting just such a revocation. Kafka has presented this type of man, who tries to recognize and vindicate the existing customs as morally true and right, in his central figure K., the land-surveyor in *The Castle.* For K.'s unremitting endeavour is to follow all the precepts, to assimilate them inwardly and to justify even the immoral claims of the rulers. In order to bring out as clearly as possible the problem raised by this attempt at justification, Kafka represents the ruling powers as evil, and the efforts of the newcomer as a dutiful determination to conform with evil: thus the conformist *acknowledges* evil as good, even though he *knows* differently. And because he knows in his heart that he cannot simply recognize as morally good whatever is commanded of him and leave the matter at that, he has a bad conscience. All Kafka's philosophical aphorisms show how he not only describes this attempt at justification, but also approves of such an equivocal undertaking, and practises it himself. He too is to some extent an apologist of conformism. The fashionable cult of Kafka is therefore to be viewed with considerable misgivings. His moral message is *sacrificium intellectus,* and his political message self-abasement.

PART TWO

View Points

The Multiplicity of Interpretations

Blake Lee Spahr

I think it would be safe to say that no single, unified critical approach to the content of Kafka's total works has been successful to date. The various attempts to assess the totality of Kafka's creation from the traditional approaches have failed. All those who claim that *their interpretation*—symbolic, allegorical, psychoanalytic, religious—[is correct] must admit that *all* the stories do not fit their approach. Either the works themselves must be twisted and forced into the preconceived mold, or the vantage point, the perspective, must be altered from work to work. The secret cabala, which Kafka once claimed (mischievously, I suspect) underlies the works, has not as yet been discovered, and all unified attempts to discover it have failed.

"The Bridge and the Abyss" by Blake Lee Spahr. From Modern Fiction Studies, *VII (Spring, 1962), 6.*

Origins of *The Castle*

Jorge Luis Borges

Once I planned to make a survey of Kafka's precursors. At first I thought he was as singular as the fabulous Phoenix; when I knew him better I thought I recognized his voice, or his habits, in the texts of various literatures and various ages. I shall record a few of them here, in chronological order.

The first is Zeno's paradox against movement. A moving body on

---

From Other Inquisitions, 1937–1952 *by Jorge Luis Borges, trans. by Ruth L. C. Simms (Austin, Texas: University of Texas Press, 1964).*

A (declares Aristotle) will not be able to reach point *B*, because before it does, it must cover half of the distance between the two, and before that, half of the half, and before that, half of the half of the half, and so on to infinity; the formula of this famous problem is, exactly, that of *The Castle;* and the moving body and the arrow and Achilles are the first Kafkian characters in literature.

Max Brod

Despite the wider, indeed religious and universal themes with which *The Castle* is concerned, the autobiographical element should not be overlooked. . . . At the present time, no more need be said than this: *The Castle* reflects, in a distorted form, Kafka's love affair with Milena, described with a curious scepticism and prejudice which perhaps offered Kafka his only way out of the crisis. Milena, who appears in caricature in the novel as "Frieda," makes determined efforts to save Kafka (K.), she unites herself to him, she sets up house with him in poverty and distress, yet gladly, deliberately, she wishes to be his for ever and so to lead him back to the freshness and immediacy of real life; but as soon as K. agrees, grasps the hand which she offers, her former associations, which dominate her, reassert themselves (the "Castle," her race, society, and above all the sinister Herr Klamm, in whom one may recognize a nightmare picture of Milena's legal husband, with whom she could never break completely), and their dreamed-of happiness comes to a sudden end; for K. will not accept compromises, and his bride, for all her good intentions, is also not one of those who try to evade the choice of "all or nothing" and who know how to find the middle way of diplomacy. At the same time it is clear that in K. the will to radical salvation is even more uncompromising than in Frieda, who burns with too insubstantial a fire and too easily gives way to disillusion. The parallel between truth and the fiction can be pursued even further, and is brought out especially in K.'s self-torturing character (he sees himself as an

---

From the "Introduction" by Max Brod to Conversations with Kafka, *by Gustav Janouch, trans. Goronwy Rees (London: Derek Verschoyle, 1953; New York: New Directions Publishing Corporation, 1969), pp. xvii–xviii.*

impostor). Milena's women friends, who dissuaded her from her choice, in the novel find their apotheosis in the legendary, fateful figure of the "Landlady," who to some extent plays the part of the chorus in Greek tragedy. Frieda's strange jealousy and contempt of Olga in the novel are the counterpart to the attitude which, according to the letters, Milena adopted towards J. W., to whom at that time Kafka was engaged. She categorically demanded that Kafka should break off all relations with W. and her family. Kafka himself regarded her demand as harsh and even unjust, but nevertheless he obeyed. Such fragments of reality are to be found throughout the novel, yet one is only inspired with even greater admiration, when one realizes that from these fragments Kafka has raised a structure which towers above them all, a work of art, ominous, obscured in twilight, prophetic, in which the writer has imaginatively re-created and re-fashioned the materials of life. The importance of autobiographical elements in the genesis of a work of art should certainly not be exaggerated; but if one entirely underestimates them, one can too easily arrive at a mistaken view.

Aesthetic Effect

James Burnham

At the literal level, it is as if Kafka pours on the body of the world a kind of acid, which dissolves all the connective tissue, leaving only the discrete elements of an organism. He then selects from among the elements according to an arbitrary will of his own, and re-unites these by ligaments spun out of his own spirit. The laws, therefore, of the world as we normally know it, do not, or need not hold. The relations of space, time, causality, identity, the divisions between dream and waking, reality and illusion, all the categories through which we stabilize—and thus also in part hide—the flux of experience are dissolved, or distorted. The ego's "reality principle" is suspended.

From "Observation on Kafka" by James Burnham, Partisan Review, *XIV, ii (1947), 190. Copyright © 1947 by* Partisan Review. *Reprinted by permission of* Partisan Review *and James Burnham.*

R. W. Flint

Since only so much of the material world as is essential to locate a spiritual reality is necessary to Kafka's art, that is all he gives us. But he does emphatically give us that much. He does describe faces, textures, "nature," character, etc., very minutely when that is necessary.

From "Kafka and the Habits of Critics: A Communication" by R. W. Flint, Partisan Review, *XIV, ii (1947), 520–21. Copyright © 1947 by* Partisan Review. *Reprinted by permission of* Partisan Review *and R. W. Flint.*

Wayne C. Booth

No one tells us in *The Castle* what K.'s goal is, or whether it is attainable, or whether it is a worthwhile goal in the first place. Our puzzlement is intended to be as great as K.'s. When Christian begins to turn aside from the unmistakably correct path, we experience unequivocal dramatic irony: we stand on a secure promontory and watch the character stumble. But when K. stumbles, we stumble with him. The ironies work against us fully as much as they do against him. In such works we do not discover until the end—and very often not even then—what the true meaning of the events has been. Regardless of the point of view in the narrowest sense, the moral and intellectual point of view of the work is deliberately confusing, disconcerting, even staggering.

From The Rhetoric of Fiction *by Wayne C. Booth (Chicago: University of Chicago Press, 1961), p. 287. Reprinted by permission of the University of Chicago Press.*

Walter Sokel

Those who think that the protagonist's perspective is the whole of Kafka are victims of the subtle deception perpetrated by it. In the two K. novels and several of the longer narratives, the protagonist's

From Franz Kafka *by Walter Sokel (New York: Columbia University Press, 1966), pp. 12–13. Copyright © 1966 by Columbia University Press. Reprinted by permission of the publisher.*

motivation is to hide the truth either from himself or from the world, including the reader. However, in most of Kafka's works the truth becomes known. The protagonist's perspective, to be sure, operates for the purpose of blocking access to and comprehension of the truth, but the truth of the story emerges through the defeat of the protagonist's consciousness. In one of his aphorisms, Kafka defined truth as the light reflected upon the retreating grimace (of falsehood) and art as the condition of being dazzled by that light. This aphorism supplies the key to Kafka's poetics, always implicit in his works. The annihilation or refutation suffered by Kafka's protagonist, bearer of the lie, becomes the negative revelation of truth.

This structural principle of Kafka's narratives explains the profound difference between Kafka's method and the stream-of-consciousness technique. The latter assumes the identity of consciousness and truth. It reveals character and, with character, the truth of the narrative. It operates within the framework of psychology. In Kafka's narratives, on the contrary, consciousness hides truth. Therefore, Kafka has to transcend psychology. His concern is not the mechanism of self, but its moral and spiritual justification. In order to express this concern, he must unmask the mechanism, and in doing that he reveals a great deal about it. Kafka is a master in uncovering the subtle workings of rationalization, subterfuge, self-deception. But for Kafka this unmasking is not the end of his art. The end is always the revelation of truth in the defeat of the self.

Early Interpretations

Coley Taylor

The Castle, beyond its environmental significance, is a bureaucracy, an institution; the difficulties that K. encounters are those any ordinary person experiences in trying to influence an institution. Klamm the inaccessible might very well be any captain of industry who has surrounded himself with secretaries and ceremonies to keep besiegers away; the Castle staff which works at cross purposes in its various departments might be any big business so overgrown that its various

---

"Review of The Castle" *by Coley Taylor,* New York Herald Tribune, Books *(September 21, 1930), p. 7.*

officials are ignorant of the work of others, or of the doings of their underlings.

Agnes W. Smith

The name of Franz Kafka is probably unknown to you. In 1925, this obscure German-Bohemian died and named his friend, Herr Max Brod, as executor of an estate that consisted principally of manuscripts, most of them unfinished. Herr Brod was ordered by the terms of the will to destroy all the manuscripts. Naturally and rightly, the executor did no such thing. An author, in judging his own works, is obviously of unsound mind.

So here, then, is "The Castle" translated into English by Edwin and Willa Muir and thrust into a world that will be baffled by its perplexities, touched and impressed by its sombre beauty and originality, and bored by that dullness which is the mark of unhappy genius. "The Castle" is an allegory of man's search for divine grace: a troublesome, complex puzzle of man's soul, which is constantly teased, thwarted, and fascinated by a supreme authority which must be placated and obeyed.

The structure of the book is extremely fine and ambitious. A Land Surveyor is summoned on a mission to a village which is dominated by the Castle. Nobody wants him when he arrives, nobody has any idea of his duties, and nobody is willing to concede that he has any business being there at all. In a haphazard way, the Castle watches over him and, in just as irrational a manner, it sets him at cross-purposes and chases him off on useless errands.

The Land Surveyor, of course, is a brother to John Bunyan's Pilgrim and a cousin to Peer Gynt. Mr. Kafka, however, while holding on to the necessary aloof atmosphere of allegory, has artfully and imaginatively made his Land Surveyor a modern figure. The hapless soul is tortured by strange telephone calls and is placed at the mercy of documents which are unaccountably mislaid in filing cabinets. The new routine of life complicates his ancient problems. God, in short, is everlastingly giving him wrong numbers.

I warn you that the book is dull. I also warn you that the allegory

---

From a review of The Castle *by "A. W. S." (Agnes W. Smith),* The New Yorker *(September 20, 1930), pp. 95–96.*

is often obscured and fogged beyond all reason. And I again warn you that the work is unfinished and so you are not repaid for your pains, as you are with "Faust," by a triumphant chorus of angel voices at the end. Moreover, although Mr. Kafka tells his story with slow suspense, he has no brilliancy of words to light you on your way. Nevertheless, there hasn't been a book this season so prayerfully planned or so earnestly written.

LATER INTERPRETATIONS

Donald Pearce

Cartesian doubt, and its idiot offspring modern scientism, dropping like a guillotine on philosophy, had severed the spiritual and the physical worlds; and by 1900 had substituted caprice and entropy for order and teleology. Instead of cosmology Kafka inherited psychology—the irrational internal universe of Freud and Jung for the rational external universe of Aristotle and Ptolemy; instead of the doctrinal calm of Aquinas, there was the subtle anguish of Kierkegaard. All these influences shaped his work; so that whereas Dante's poem might be called a philosophical and theological treatise, *The Castle* is a case book in abnormal psychology; or if the former is a philosophic allegory, the latter is a modern *Psychomachia.*

From "The Castle: *Kafka's Divine Comedy," in* Franz Kafka Today, *eds. Angel Flores and Homer Swander (Madison: University of Wisconsin Press, 1962), pp. 166–67. Reprinted with permission of the copyright owners, the Regents of the University of Wisconsin.*

Charles Neider

I am willing to agree that K.'s efforts to become a member of the village community represent a search for grace, for belonging, but I can't agree that the Castle represents either the dispensation of grace or the divine. In not one instance does the Castle manifest real power; its power is purely suggestive, it resides only in the superstitions of the villagers; in this sense it is similar to the Courts

From "Franz Kafka and the Cabalists" by Charles Neider, Quarterly Review of Literature, *II, No. 3 (1945), p. 257. Copyright 1945 by T. Weiss. Reprinted by permission of* Quarterly Review of Literature.

of *The Trial.* Only the villagers can dispense grace, only they can accept or ostracize. Therefore the irony of the novel, as well as the implied criticism of the "divine" school, lies in the fact that K.'s sole possibility for grace rests in himself, in his willingness to become like the villagers in order to be accepted by them, in his readiness to accept the village superstitions, the Castle cabalism. In short, he must give up his dependence on justice related to logic. Obviously this is not what Kafka advocated; therefore the book can be read only as a satire on what he did *not* advocate, a satire on the particular search for grace which K. represents. This the mystical school does not see, since it is blinded, by its obsession with the Castle as the divine, into as ready an acceptance of the Castle cabalism as the villagers themselves. The mystical interpreters, in short, manage to adjust themselves very nicely to the village; and it is they who find the state of grace, not K. Nor does the fact that Kafka yearned to belong controvert my explanation. At the same time that he yearned to belong he despised belonging.

Walter Kaufmann

In the usual exegesis, Kafka's castle stands for God: the hero is remote from God, while the people in the village are nearer to God, and the problem is one of divine grace. At the beginning of the novel, however, we are told that the castle is the castle of Count Westwest, and after that the count no longer figures in the story. The German *"west"* means "decomposes." I suggest that in *The Castle* God is dead, and we are faced with a universe devoid of sense.

From Existentialism from Dostoevsky to Sartre, *ed. Walter Kaufmann (New York: The World Publishing Company, Meridian Books, 1956), p. 122.*

Hans Joachim Schoeps

. . . The ultimate reason for K.'s failure is perhaps only this, that he cannot have faith and commits the error of trying to force Grace

---

From "The Tragedy of Faithlessness" by Hans Joachim Schoeps in The Kafka Problem, *ed. Angel Flores (New York: New Directions Publishing Corp.), pp. 289–90.*

upon himself. For he lacked one thing during all his struggles, during all his life: the pious conviction, the hopeful confidence that what the castle would give him would be that which he considered good for him—that which eternity finds good. Therefore, because of his impatience, the castle refuses to receive him during his life. When he finally breaks down, K. gains the painful insight. "He who searches, finds not; he who does not search, is found."

Frederick Hoffman

The great difference of opinion which Kafka had with psychoanalysis in the matter of religion and ethics can be demonstrated in no better way than by reference to the story of Abraham's trial. Considered from the point of view of social ethics, Abraham's intention must be thought of as murderous. With this conclusion Kierkegaard would certainly have agreed. For to slay one's son, if one does not have faith in God's decree—absurd as that decree may appear—is actually to commit murder. It has no spiritual justification and has therefore to be judged in a secular court. The psychoanalyst would dwell upon the absurdity of the notion and would consider Abraham's religious justification of it as an enormous and dangerous illusion. He would probably have committed Abraham to an asylum, as a dangerous incurable, and would be justified in so doing, in terms of his scientific evaluation of motives and behavior.[1] Kafka played whimsically with the theme.[2] He studied Kierkegaard's book carefully during the time when he was composing *The Castle*. In this novel he develops Kierkegaard's thesis most fully in the story of the Barnabas family. Amalia has angrily refused to accept an order from Sortini, which she regards as absurd and loathsome. As a consequence, quite without

---

From Freudianism and the Literary Mind *by Frederick Hoffman (Baton Rouge: Louisiana State University Press, 1957), pp. 202–3.*

[1] American treatment of this theme is to be found in Sherwood Anderson's story "Godliness," in *Winesburg, Ohio,* 55–87. Jesse Bentley tries to offer up his son David as a sacrifice to God, but David escapes. Bentley fails because his faith is anchored in material wishes, and he expects the sacrifice to be rewarded. See especially *ibid.,* 86–87.

[2] See Kafka to Robert Klopstock, in Slochower *et al., A Franz Kafka Miscellany,* 73–74. See also Franz Kafka, "Fragment: Four Sagas Tell About Prometheus," in *Transition,* XXIII (1935), 25, where he discusses four possible versions of the Prometheus story.

any deliberate action on the part of Sortini, who has probably forgotten the incident altogether, Amalia and her family lose their position in the Village, are looked down upon, and Amalia is forced to take upon herself the burden of caring for her prematurely aged parents. Amalia's act of refusal is right and reasonable, so K. tells her. That is in accordance with rational standards. Amalia, however, eventually senses the truth that her act was a defiance of the demands of faith—demands which are loathsome, incredible, and repulsive. Kafka is attempting to say here, and elsewhere, that one cannot judge the demands of one's God in terms of rational being. It is in the acceptance of the irrational that one transcends rational ethics and enters into a hitherto inexplicable relationship with God.

Roy Pascal

K.'s tragedy is that his goal is unattainable because it appears to him only under the form of an illusion. He cannot remain isolated, for the freedom of isolation is meaningless. But he cannot accept a community at any price, with its false values and fetishes. So he remains in a border region between community and isolation. Kafka himself was in such a position, between the Czech, German and Jewish communities, between bourgeoisie and proletariat, an isolation intensified by his illness which took him to one sanatorium after another. "This border region between loneliness and community I have crossed extremely rarely, I have even settled in it more than in loneliness itself." [1]

From The German Novel *by Roy Pascal (Manchester, England: Manchester University Press, 1956), pp. 243–44. Copyright 1956 Manchester University Press. Reprinted by permission of the publisher.*

John Urzidil

There hardly exists a more stirring portrayal of Jewish loneliness in the midst of an ostracizing world than Kafka's novel *The*

From "Franz Kafka: Novelist and Mystic" by John Urzidil, The Menorah Journal, *XXX, No. 1 (1943), pp. 273–78. Copyright Johannes Urzidil. Reprinted by permission of the author.*

[1] *Tagebücher* (ed. 1937), pp. 109–10.

Castle. It is not stated that the hero of the book, a surveyor, is a Jew. The other persons portrayed are not described as hostile or even envious. None of them wants to do anything at all to the surveyor, who makes vain efforts without number to overcome his foreignness and become a member of the community. But he can neither gain entry into the castle nor be accepted in the village. Nobody invites him, nobody throws him out. No one shows him the door, no one detains him. Here is the symbol of Jewry's foreignness and loneliness in the *Galuth.*

Hannah Arendt

The outstanding characteristics of the K. in *The Castle* is that he is interested only in universals, in those things to which all men have a natural right. But while he demands no more than this, it is quite obvious that he will be satisfied with nothing less. He is easily enough persuaded to change his profession, but an occupation, "regular work," he demands as his right. The troubles of K. start because only the Castle can fulfill his demands; and the Castle will do this either as an "act of favor" or if he consents to become its secret employee —"an ostensible village worker whose real occupation is determined through Barnabas," the court messenger.

Since his demands are nothing more than the inalienable rights of man, he cannot accept them as an "act of favor from the Castle." At this point the villagers step in; they try to persuade K. that he lacks experience and does not know that the whole of life is constituted and dominated by favor and disfavor, by grace and disgrace, both as inexplicable, as hazardous as good and bad luck. To be in the right or in the wrong, they try to explain to him, is part of "fate" which no one can alter, which one can only fulfill.

K.'s strangeness therefore receives an additional meaning: he is strange not only because he does not "belong to the village, and does not belong to the Castle," but because he is the only normal and healthy human being in a world where everything human and normal, love and work and fellowship, has been wrested out of men's hands to become a gift endowed from without—or as Kafka puts it,

---

From "Franz Kafka: A Revaluation" by Hannah Arendt, Partisan Review, *XI (Fall, 1944), pp. 415–16.*

from above. Whether as fate, as blessing or as curse, it is something mysterious, something which man may receive or be denied, but never can create. Accordingly, K.'s aspirations, far from being commonplace and obvious, is, in fact, exceptional and scandalous. He puts up a fight for the minimum as if it were something which embraced the sum total of all possible demands. For the villagers K.'s strangeness consists not of his being deprived of the essentials of life but of his asking for them.

K.'s stubborn singleness of purpose, however, opens the eyes of some of the villagers; his behavior teaches them that human rights may be worth fighting for, that the rule of the Castle is not divine law and, consequently, can be attacked. He makes them see, as they put it, that "men who suffered our kind of experiences, who are beset by our kind of fear . . . who tremble at every knock at the door, cannot see things straight." And they add: "How lucky are we that you came to us!" The fight of the stranger, however, had no other result than his being an example. His struggle ends with a death of exhaustion—a perfectly natural death. But since he, unlike the K. of *The Trial,* did not submit to what appeared as necessity there is no shame to outlive him.

Homer Swander

Most responsible critics, from Marxists to Catholics, while disagreeing on other matters, continue to accept with no essential change the semiofficial interpretations of Max Brod and Thomas Mann in which the village represents "life, the soil, the community, healthy normal existence and the blessings of human and bourgeois society," and in which K. is seen as "driven on . . . by a need for the most primitive requisites of life, the need to be rooted in a home and a calling, and to become a member of a community." [1] Or, as R. O. C. Winkler has put it more absolutely, "the hero's whole efforts are directed immediately toward an attempt to establish himself in a home and a job,

---

From "The Castle: *K.'s Village" by Homer Swander, in* Franz Kafka Today, *eds. Angel Flores and Homer Swander (Madison: The University of Wisconsin Press, 1962), pp. 174, 185, 192. Reprinted with permission of the copyright owners, the Regents of the University of Wisconsin.*

[1] Thomas Mann, "Homage," *The Castle* (New York, 1954), p. xiv; Max Brod, "Additional Note," *The Castle* (New York, 1946), p. 330.

and to become a member of the village community—to come to terms, in fact, with society." [2]

If Brod were correct in saying that a home, job, and village citizenship are "simply the right life, the right way (Tao)," [3] then K., the stranger, would presumably show some passionately active desire to be a stranger no longer. He would, at the very least, envy the villagers. His struggle would seem to him the fight of a lone man to become one among many, not a fight that can only be waged—or, incredibly, won—alone. Yet we remember that K. became a stranger by choice, that he came to this village from his native town—and now remains here—of his "own accord." And we find that almost never in the entire novel does K. feel drawn toward any individual unless he believes that that individual can, specifically and directly, help him to get into the Castle or to confront Klamm.

Conclusion

Herbert Tauber

The end planned for the novel seems to move in the same set of circumstances as all that has gone before. In his first epilogue Max Brod informs us: "Kafka never wrote his concluding chapter. But he told me about it once when I asked him how the novel was to end. The

[2] R. O. C. Winkler, "The Three Novels," *The Kafka Problem,* ed. Angel Flores (New York, 1946), p. 194. Harry Slochower, *No Voice Is Wholly Lost* (New York, 1945), p. 114, writes of "The Communal Castle." Walter J. Ong, "Kafka's Castle in the West," *Thought,* XXII (Sept., 1947), p. 460, says "that whatever goes for [the village] goes for everything." Charles Neider, "The Cabalists," *Kafka Problem,* p. 429, agrees with Brod "that K.'s efforts to become a member of the village community represent a search for grace, for belonging," and says (p. 435) that "the village acts as a microcosm. . . ." W. H. Auden, "K.'s Quest," *Kafka Problem,* p. 50, believes "the hero of *The Castle* wants to be allowed to settle down in the village." Nathan A. Scott, *Rehearsals of Discomposure* (New York, 1952), p. 50, says, "The Village is, of course, existence, the world. . . ." Herbert Tauber, *Franz Kafka: An Interpretation of his Works,* tr. by G. Humphreys Roberts and Roger Senhouse (New Haven, 1948), p. 133, believes that "for K. the village is worldly reality, into which it is a question of being co-ordinated somehow or other," and adds (p. 138) that "the village is a symbol of human life. . . ." Other examples are plentiful; but these will perhaps suggest the wide variety of critics who, in their understanding of K.'s relationship with the village, do not differ basically from Brod and Mann.

[3] Max Brod, *The Castle* (1946), p. 330.

ostensible Land Surveyor was to find partial satisfaction at least. He was not to relax in his struggle, but was only to die worn out by it. Round his deathbed the villagers were to assemble, and from the Castle itself the word was to come that though K.'s legal claim to live in the village was not valid, yet, taking certain coincident circumstances into account, he was to be permitted to live and work there."

. . . The irony is softened by the fact that K. is surrounded by the villagers at the moment of his death. Even if his life was that of a foreigner, he now dies as a member of the community. Thereby the word that is directed towards him does not fall into empty space. It is at the same time a message to the community: the foreigner possessed with the spirit of endless striving is confirmed as one of them. His suffering and defeat receive a kind of exemplary character—not, of course, in the sense of a model—but rather as a kind of public sacrifice which has perished vicariously at the hands of the unsolved character of the earth.

Kafka himself surely sacrificed this creation of his soul vicariously. In it he allowed to be wrecked that rebellious and self-distinctive spirit, wavering between nihilism and magic, in order to step back from the frightened and yet defiant "I" pronouncement of K.'s into the circle of the community and its "we." That is, admittedly, a "we" that dare no longer shut out the stranger in sullen self-righteousness, but must count him—as a stranger—as one of them.

From Franz Kafka: An Interpretation of his Works *by Herbert Tauber, trans. by G. Humphreys Roberts and Roger Senhouse (New Haven: Yale University Press; London: Martin Secker & Warburg, Ltd., 1948), pp. 183–85.*

Paul Goodman

In a bald diagram the structure of *The Castle* is as follows. There is a turmoil of conflicting plots in two sets; K.'s purpose and the high authorities; and the village, Frieda, and the women of Barnabas—and this turmoil is so managed and so kept in motion by the protagonist's character and fixing disposition that it can never come to an end. Meantime there is a series of lyrical passages that point to a resolution. The catastrophe is the final exhaustion of the protagonist, in death, putting

---

From The Structure of Literature *by Paul Goodman (Chicago: The University of Chicago Press, 1962), pp. 182–83.*

to a stop the motion of the turmoil without an issue either way. But the dénouement, never written, should be the full expression of the lyrical resolution passages. The pattern of the book then is to exhaust the watchful, wilful, and stubborn protagonist and carry him away with the satisfaction that comes with finally giving in.

Chronology of Important Dates

	Kafka	*The Age*
1860–1904		Hauptmann, Suderman, Schnitzler, Chekhov writing.
1882		Charles Darwin dies.
1883	Kafka born, July 3, in Prague.	Karl Marx, Richard Wagner die.
1898		Early Thomas Mann stories published.
1899		Boer War.
1902	Meets Max Brod.	
1906	Doctorate in Law.	
Pre-1907	Wrote "Description of a Struggle," and "Wedding Preparations in the Country."	
1908	Begins employment with Workers' Accident Insurance Institute.	
1910	Friendship with Yiddish Theater troupe in Prague.	
1912	Begins *Der Verschollene* (*Amerika*); meets Felice Bauer; writes *The Metamorphosis.*	
1914	Begins *The Trial.* Engagement to F. B. June 11, "Temptation in the Village" in *Diaries.* This is a preliminary sketch for *The Castle.*	World War I begins.
1917	Tuberculosis verified. Reads Kierkegaard. Lives with his sister, Ottla, in Zürau, and makes *Diary* notes on lives of farmers.	

1918		Armistice. Oswald Spengler's *Decline of the West*; Kaiser's *Gas*.
1919	Publication of *A Country Doctor* and *In the Penal Colony*. Writes *Letter to his Father*.	
1920	Meets Milena Jesenská.	
1922	Reads opening chapter of *The Castle* to Brod.	James Joyce's *Ulysses*.
1923	Friendship with Dora Dymant, Berlin and Prague.	Inflation. Financial catastrophe in Germany.
1924	Publication of collection, *A Hunger Artist*. Dies, June 3, in sanatorium at Kierling, near Vienna, with Robert Klopstock and Dora Dymant present.	Joseph Conrad dies. Thomas Mann's *The Magic Mountain*.
1926	Publication of *The Castle*.	

Notes on the Editor and Contributors

PETER F. NEUMEYER, the editor of this collection, received his Ph.D. from the University of California, and now teaches at Harvard. He has published poetry and numerous articles, and his first children's book will be published January 1969.

GÜNTHER ANDERS, poet, essayist, philosopher, has written about George Grosz, Brecht, and Kafka, as well as about the immorality of nuclear warfare.

HANNAH ARENDT, author, political scientist, and professor at the University of Chicago, has written many books. Among them *The Origins of Totalitarianism* (1951) and *The Human Condition* (1958).

WAYNE BOOTH, Professor of English, and dean of the College, University of Chicago, was a Guggenheim fellow 1956–1957, received the Christian Gauss Prize of Phi Beta Kappa, and is a member of the board of trustees of Earlham College.

JORGE LUIS BORGES, born in Buenos Aires in 1899, and educated in Europe, is director of the National Library of Argentina and Professor of English Literature at the University of Buenos Aires.

MAX BROD, himself a noted novelist, was Kafka's lifelong friend, and, after Kafka's death, became his literary executor and editor.

JAMES BURNHAM, graduate of Oxford and Princeton, has written numerous books: among them, *The Web of Subversion* (1954), *Congress and the American Tradition* (1959), and *Suicide of the West* (1964).

HENRI DANIEL-ROPS, French writer, historian, member of the French Academy, Chevalier of the Legion of Honor, has written novels, and numerous works of church history, in addition to editing the journal, *Ecclesia*.

R. W. FLINT wrote many reviews for *Partisan Review* in the late 'forties and early 'fifties.

PAUL GOODMAN, author of poems, literary studies, book reviews, and iconoclastic social criticism such as *Growing Up Absurd* (1956), is also author of *Kafka's Prayer* (New York, 1947).

ERICH HELLER is the author of *The Disinherited Mind* and *The Ironic German: A Study of Thomas Mann*. He has taught in England, and is presently Professor of German at Northwestern University.

FREDERICK HOFFMAN was Professor of English at the University of California at Riverside, and at the University of Wisconsin. He wrote extensively on twentieth century British and American literature.

WALTER KAUFMANN is Professor of Philosophy at Princeton. Among his numerous books are *Twenty German Poets: a bilingual edition* (1962) and *The Birth of Tragedy and the Case of Wagner* (1967).

The late EDWIN MUIR, with his wife Willa Muir, translated Kafka's novels into English. He was a poet and novelist, as well as the author of an autobiography, *The Story and the Fable.*

CHARLES NEIDER has ranged widely in his writing on literary topics. His work includes studies of Thomas Mann, Mark Twain, as well as *The Frozen Sea: A Study of Franz Kafka.*

FREDERICK A. OLAFSON has taught at Stanford, and is presently Professor of Education and Philosophy at Harvard. In 1961 he published *Society, Law and Morality.*

ROY PASCAL, Professor of German at Birmingham (England) University since 1931, has written may books, including *The Growth of Modern Germany* (1946).

DONALD R. PEARCE, scholar, novelist, and poet, is Professor of English at the University of California at Santa Barbara. His latest book is *In the President's and My Opinion* (Prentice-Hall, 1968).

HEINZ POLITZER, Vienna-born critic and scholar, has taught, among other places, at Bryn Mawr, Oberlin, and Cornell. Presently he is Professor of German at the University of California (Berkeley).

HANS JOACHIM SCHOEPS has written numerous historical studies of the Prussian state, on Judaism and Christianity, and on literary and historical figures. *The Jewish-Christian Argument; a history of theologies in conflict* (1963) is one of the few works translated into English.

AGNES W. SMITH, who wrote the early *New Yorker* review of *The Castle,* was the sister of Sally Benson, a writer for *The New Yorker.*

WALTER SOKEL, formerly of Columbia, is now Professor of German at Stanford University. Among other books, he has written *The Writer in Extremis: Expressionism in Twentieth-Century German Literature.*

BLAKE LEE SPAHR, Professor of German at the University of California (Berkeley), is the author of *Anton Ulrich and Aramena; the genesis and development of a baroque novel* (1966).

ERWIN RAY STEINBERG, Dean of the Margaret Morrison Carnegie College of the Carnegie Institute of Technology, and formerly a Coordinator for Project English, writes about the novel and about the teaching of English.

HOMER SWANDER, together with Angel Flores, edited the excellent selection of essays, *Franz Kafka Today* (1962).

HERBERT TAUBER is a Swiss scholar, journalist, and novelist. His book, *Franz Kafka: An Interpretation of his Works,* has been published by the Yale University Press.

COLEY TAYLOR, together with Saul Middlebrook, wrote *The Eagle Screams* (1936), a book about political polemics. He also wrote *Mark Twain's Margins on Thackeray's "Swift"* (1935).

JOHN URZIDIL grew up in the Prague of Franz Kafka, Max Brod, and Franz Werfel. He has lived in England and the United States, and is the author of novels, memoirs, and poetry.

Selected Bibliography

BIBLIOGRAPHY

Serious study of Franz Kafka must necessarily begin with either of the two excellent Kafka bibliographies. The one by Hemmerle covers Kafka's own writings too.

Hemmerle, Rudolf. *Franz Kafka. Eine Bibliographie.* München: Verlag Robert Lerche, 1958.

Järv, Harry. *Die Kafka-Literatur. Eine Bibliographie.* Mälmo & Lund, Bo Cavefors, 1961.

BIOGRAPHY AND CRITICISM

Brod, Max. *Franz Kafka: A Biography.* Trans. G. Humphreys Roberts and Richard Winston. New York: Schocken Books, 1960 (second, enlarged adition). This is the basic biography, by Kafka's close friend and literary executor.

Emrich, Wilhelm. *Franz Kafka.* Bonn: Athenäum, 1958. An exhaustive biographical and critical study, in German.

Flores, Angel and Homer Swander, eds. *Franz Kafka Today.* Madison: University of Wisconsin Press, 1958. An excellent, selected bibliography, as well as a diverse selection of important essays.

Gray, Ronald. *Kafka's Castle.* Cambridge: Cambridge University Press, 1956. The only entire volume dedicated solely to *The Castle,* a short book representing its author's very individual interpretation.

Gray, Ronald, ed. *Kafka: A Collection of Critical Essays.* Englewood Cliffs: Prentice-Hall, Inc., 1962.

Politzer, Heinz. *Franz Kafka: Parable and Paradox.* Ithaca: Cornell University Press, 1962. The only book-length interpretation in English of all Kafka's writing, accounting for its origins and analyzing its recurring images and central paradoxes.

Sokel, Walter H. *Franz Kafka.* New York and London: Columbia University Press, 1966. An inexpensive and useful introduction for the student new to Kafka, with a good, brief bibliography.

Sokel, Walter H. *Franz Kafka. Tragik und Ironie. Zur Struktur seiner Kunst.* München und Wien: Albert Langen-Georg Müller, 1964. A major critical interpretation of Kafka's writings.

Wagenbach, Klaus. *Franz Kafka. Eine Biographie seiner Jugend. 1883–1912.* Bern: Francke, 1958. An excellent, short, paperback biographical introduction to Kafka, containing many quotations, numerous fascinating photographs of Kafka, his friends, and his surroundings, as well as a useful bibliography.

TWENTIETH CENTURY INTERPRETATIONS

MAYNARD MACK, *Series Editor*
Yale University

NOW AVAILABLE
Collections of Critical Essays
ON

ADVENTURES OF HUCKLEBERRY FINN
ALL FOR LOVE
ARROWSMITH
AS YOU LIKE IT
BLEAK HOUSE
THE BOOK OF JOB
THE CASTLE
DUBLINERS
THE DUCHESS OF MALFI
EURIPIDES' ALCESTIS
THE FROGS
GRAY'S ELEGY
THE GREAT GATSBY
GULLIVER'S TRAVELS
HAMLET
HENRY IV, PART TWO
HENRY V
THE ICEMAN COMETH
JULIUS CAESAR
KEATS'S ODES
OEDIPUS REX
THE OLD MAN AND THE SEA
PAMELA
THE PORTRAIT OF A LADY
A PORTRAIT OF THE ARTIST AS A YOUNG MAN

Samson Agonistes
The Scarlet Letter
Sir Gawain and the Green Knight
The Sound and the Fury
Tom Jones
Twelfth Night
Utopia
Walden
The Waste Land
Wuthering Heights

3 5132 00428 1622
University of the Pacific Library